The Letters of Pierre de Cros, Chamberlain to Pope Gregory XI (1371–1378)

Medieval and Renaissance
Texts and Studies
Volume 356

The Letters of Pierre de Cros, Chamberlain to Pope Gregory XI (1371–1378)

BY

Daniel Williman

ACMRS
(Arizona Center for Medieval and Renaissance Studies)
Tempe, Arizona
2009

© Copyright 2009
Arizona Board of Regents for Arizona State University

Library of Congress Cataloging-in-Publication Data

Pierre, de Cros, 1322-1388.
  The letters of Pierre de Cros, chamberlain to Pope Gregory XI, 1371-1378 / by Daniel Williman.
      p. cm. -- (Medieval and renaissance texts and studies ; v. 356)
  Includes bibliographical references and index.
  ISBN 978-0-86698-404-1 (alk. paper)
  1. Pierre, de Cros, 1322-1388--Correspondence. 2. Gregory XI, Pope, 1329-1378. 3. Catholic Church--History. I. Williman, Daniel. II. Title.

BX4705.P47348A4 2008
282.092--dc22

2008030887

∞
This book is made to last.
It is set in Adobe Caslon Pro,
smyth-sewn and printed on acid-free paper
to library specifications.
Printed in the United States of America

Table of Contents

Figures — vii

Preface — ix

Abbreviated Citations — xi

Coinages and Accounts — xiii

Weights and Measures — xvii

1. The Life and Family of Pierre de Cros — 1
   A. Ecclesiastical Career — 1
   B. Family Connections — 6
   C. Testaments and Succession of Pierre de Cros — 13

2. Administration of the Camera Apostolica 1371-1378 — 17
   A. The Chamberlain as Judge — 17
   B. Personnel and Administration of the Camera — 23
   C. Fiscal Resources of the Apostolic See — 39

3. The Ministerial Policies of Pierre de Cros — 47
   A. Government of Avignon — 47
   B. Holy Thursday Anathema — 51
   C. War Policy — 53
   D. Return of the Curia to Italy — 66

4. The Sources and the Calendar — 73
   A. Diplomatic Sketch — 73
   B. The Seal and Signet of Pierre de Cros — 74
   C. Sources in the Vatican Archives — 76

Appendix I: The *Itinerarium* of Pierre Ameilh — 81

Appendix II: Family Relations of Pope Gregory XI — 89

Bibliography — 99

Index — 111

Figures

1.1	Select Genealogy: De Cros and Roger	10
2.1	Pope's Tower in Section, Viewed from the South	20
2.2	Plan of the Palace at Avignon: The Treasury Area	22
2.3	Upper Treasury and Great Library	25
2.4	Carlin or Gros of Gregory XI	31
2.5	Cameral Florin of Gregory XI	32
4.1	The Great Seal and Signet of Pierre de Cros	75
Appendix	Select Genealogy: Roger and Allied Families	94–97

Preface

Pierre de Cros, as chamberlain of Pope Gregory XI from 1371 to 1378, was responsible for most of the worldly wealth of the Roman Church and for much of the activity of that international state which was not related (or only accidentally related) to its religious character. His official correspondence is of great interest for political, economic, and social history, and fortunately many of his letters were registered in the offices of the Camera Apostolica at Avignon before being dispatched. Those letters are the subject and most of the content of this book. It is true that Pierre de Cros continued as chamberlain after the death of Gregory XI, through the two elections of 1378, and into the pontificate of Clement VII of Avignon, until he was made cardinal in 1383. But the circumstances of his service changed completely with the death of Gregory XI, and his later correspondence will be the matter of another volume.

    My collaborator in research, Karen Corsano, began to help with this book even before becoming my wife. She has read the Introduction in at least five instars, constantly improving its clarity and accuracy, and proofread from microfilm most of the editions of letters. Msgr. Charles Burns, a helpful friend of my research from its first days in the Vatican Archives, provided invaluable guidance to the records and expert information on certain peculiar institutions, especially the honorary swords and the chaplains of honor. Michel and Anne-Marie Hayez welcomed me several times to their home, beginning in the time when this was in the Papal Palace at Avignon and, in the perfect research partnership, they directed the Departmental Archives and the historical center there. They have been unfailingly generous advisors and supporters, patient and scrupulous readers and editors for this as for several earlier projects. Between them they have rectified many scores of mistaken place names, family relations, and institutional descriptions in this volume. Patrick Zutshi, archivist of Cambridge University, supplied several documents relevant to Pierre de Cros and crucially important for this study. He also read the entire Calendar, to the great improvement of its accuracy. But his major contribution to this book has been his example of moderation in drawing historical conclusions from questionable and incomplete data, a model which I have imperfectly followed. My study of the Camera Apostolica of Avignon began almost forty years ago in the Diplomatics seminar of Leonard Boyle at the Pontifical Institute of Mediaeval Studies in Toronto, and I am happy once again to acknowledge how much I owe Father Boyle for his instruction, his inspiration, and his example.

Daniel Williman
Cambridge, Massachusetts
March 2007

Abbreviated Citations

More complete notices are given in the Bibliography.

Albanès	Joseph M. H. Albanès, *Gallia Christiana Novissima*.
ASV	Archivio Segreto Vaticano, series:
	AA Archivum Arcis
	Coll. Collectoriae
	IM Instrumenta miscellanea
	RA Registra avenionensia
	RV Registra vaticana
Aubert Calendar	Daniel Williman, *Calendar of the Letters of Arnaud Aubert, Camerarius Apostolicus (1361-1371)*. Toronto, 1992.
Baluze-Mollat	Etienne Baluze, *Vitae paparum avenionensium...*, ed. Guillaume Mollat.
BNF	Bibliothèque nationale de France
Calendar	The Calendar of Letters of Pierre de Cros on the compact disk enclosed with this book.
DHGE	*Dictionnaire d'histoire et de géographie ecclésiastiques.*
EFR	Ecoles françaises d'Athènes et de Rome, Bibliothèque, 3e série: Registres des papes du 14e siècle, particularly
	EFR *Grégoire XI communes*
	EFR *Grégoire XI secrètes autres*
	EFR *Grégoire XI secrètes France*
	EFR *Urbain V communes*
	EFR *Urbain V secrètes France*
Eubel	Conrad Eubel, *Hierarchia catholica medii aevi*, vol. 1: *1198-1431*.
GC	*Gallia Christiana*, 2nd ed. Rome-Paris, 1870.
Samaran-Mollat	Charles Samaran and Guillaume Mollat, *La fiscalité pontificale en France au XIVe siècle*. Paris, 1905.
Suppliques	data from ASV, *Registra supplicationum* of Urban V as compiled by Anne-Marie Hayez; the volume number is followed by the serial number of the petition.

Theiner   Augustin Theiner, *Codex diplomaticus dominii temporalis S. Sedis.*

VQ 6   K. H. Schäfer, *Die Ausgaben der apostolischen Kammer unter den Päpsten Urban V. und Gregor XI. (1362-1378).* Vatikanische Quellen 6. Paderborn, 1937.

X   *Corpus Juris Canonici 2: Decretales Gregorii IX.*

Coinages and Accounts

The variety of moneys mentioned in the Calendar can be reduced to understandable order by means of two guides: Peter Spufford, *Handbook of Medieval Exchange* (London, 1986); and K. H. Schäfer, "Wertvergleiche des Florentiner Goldguldens zu den Edelmetallen und den wichtigsten europäischen Gold-, Silber- und Scheidemünzen im 13. und 14. Jahrhundert," in *Vatikanische Quellen* 2 (Paderborn, 1912), 38*-131*.

The international standard of monetary value was the gold florin of Florence, 3.53 grams of 24-karat gold. Other mints imitated the florin in weight and fineness and sometimes in pattern as well; the Cameral florin was the outstanding example. A florin of the Florentine standard was sometimes called *florenus sententie*, whether the name reflected a Florentine ordinance (Schäfer, 53*) or a papal one (Spufford, 125). Officially, one such florin was worth 26 sous of Avignon. The "current" florin, a lighter florin struck by the papal mint and others after 1371, was worth 12 gros of Provence or 24 sous of Avignon (Spufford, 125). The *florenus de grayleto* or *florenus de cornu* was minted by the prince of Orange (Schäfer, 59*) and worth only 22 sous of Avignon or less. The florin of Aragon weighed 3.48 grams of 18-karat gold, and so was worth 3/4 of a florin of Florence (Spufford, 148). The *genovino d'oro* or ducat was practically equivalent to the Florentine florin (Schäfer, 51*; Spufford, 109). The *florenus Alamannie* or *Rheingulden* was worth a Florentine florin or more (Schäfer, 55*; Spufford, 240).

The obsolescent *mouton* or *agnus auri*, first minted by Philip IV of France, was worth slightly more than a florin (Schäfer, 48*). The "florin of France" was an *écu* (Spufford, 172). The French *cathedra* or *chaise à l'écu*, commonly called *écu* or in Latin *scutum*, was the first French gold coin to appear in large quantities (Spufford, 189). The *scuta Johannis* or *écus* of King John mentioned in the accounts were received for 35 sous of Avignon. For *scuta antiqua* or *escudos* of Portugal, see below.

The French *franc à cheval*, struck from 1360 on, was 3.89 grams of 24-karat gold, originally equal in value to the silver pound of Tours. The *franc à pied*, which supplanted the *cheval* from 1365, weighed 3.82 grams and was still officially worth one pound Tours (Spufford, 191). This was the coin called *regalis auri* in the accounts. The franc was worth more than the Cameral florin by 5 to 4.

The principal English gold coin of this period was a double florin called the noble, specifically designated *nobilis de nave*, stably valued at 1/3 pound sterling or 1/2 mark sterling (Spufford, 198), and received for 2 florins of the Camera plus 5 sous of Avignon (Schäfer, 65*). *Nobiles de rosa* were small imitations of this coin, slightly over half its value, minted at Geneva. *Leopardi* were gold money of English Bordeaux (Schäfer, 64*), worth 40 pence sterling in 1360, when the florin of Florence was worth 36.

The *dupla* or *dobla*, the standard gold coin of Castile, inspired by the Moorish double dinar (Spufford, 159), was worth 35 sous of Avignon (Schäfer, 52*). I suppose the *gentilis* of Portugal (Calendar no. 512) also to be a *dobla*, and the *scuta* of Portugal to be *reis* (Spufford, 162). The *dobla morisca*, coined in Morocco, was more valuable than the Cameral florin by 5 to 4. A women's monastery of Angers (Calendar no. 217) owed a census anciently assessed in besants, for one of which the Camera would take 2/3 florin (Schäfer, 50*).

Most of the silver coins in these accounts were pennies: *denarii* or *deniers*, twelve of which constituted a *solidus* or *sou*, but that value was not a coin. Twenty *solidi* scored a pound, *libra,* or *livre,* also not a coin. In this Calendar the formula £5.19.11 is used for sums of silver in pounds, *sous,* and *deniers.* Certain systems of account used the standard gold coin in place of the theoretical pound. The Apostolic Camera calculated by florins, with fractions in *sous* and *deniers* of Avignon. The silver penny produced by the papal mint was a carlin or *iulhat*, imitating the coinage of Charles II of Anjou which had lilies on the reverse (Spufford, 62), but sometimes called a *gros* to distinguish it from baser fractional coins called *pitte* in the accounts.

These other types of silver money also appear:

— Genoese, exchanged at £1.5.0 to the Cameral florin (Spufford, 106)

— Imperial money of Milan (Schäfer, 97*; Spufford, 96).

— French royal silver of Tours (Spufford, 172).

— French royal silver of Paris (Schäfer, 106*; Spufford, 167).

— Sterling pennies of England, accounted 240 to the pound or 160 to the mark or 80 to the gold noble (Schäfer, 116*; Spufford, 198).

— *Coronats*, royal money of Provence minted at Marseille (Spufford, 117).

— *Bolognini*, rated officially at 32 *soldi* to the florin of Florence (Spufford, 72).

— *Dineros* of Barcelona, exchanged 12 or 16 *sueldos* to the florin of Florence (Schäfer, 75*; Spufford, 139).

— *Deniers bordelais,* also called money of Aquitaine or of Guienne (Spufford, 207).

— Royal *dineros* of Aragon, named *jaccenses* after Jaca, where they were originally minted (Spufford, 147).

— *Dineros carlins*, money of Navarre under Charles II the Bad (Spufford, 163).

— *Dinheiros* of Portugal (Schäfer, 110*; Spufford, 162).

— *Stephanini*, an obsolete Burgundian coinage (Schäfer, 116).

— *Morlani*, antique silver deniers of Morlaix in Brittany (Schäfer, 101*).

— German *pfennige* were 12 to the *schilling*, 12 *schillinge* to the mark (Spufford, 235).

— in Castile, the *maravedi* of account (named after the obsolete gold *morabetinos*) were equal to 10 *dineros* (Spufford, 158).

— *dineros reales* of Majorca (Spufford, 153).

Weights and Measures

English cognates of the Latin names for weights and measures, if such exist, have been adopted in this volume. Latin versions are given below in parentheses. The most useful single guide is R. E. Zupko, *French Weights and Measures Before the Revolution: A Dictionary of Provincial and Local Units* (Bloomington, 1978).

Mark (*marcha*), a weight of silver or gold, about a quarter-kilogram: Zupko, 103.

For gold, 1 mark was 24 carats of 32 grains each: 768 grains.

For silver, 1 mark was 12 pennyweight or *deniers* of 24 grains each: 288 grains.

Quintal (*quintale*), a weight of 100 pounds (*libre*) or almost 50 kilograms: Zupko, 154.

Seam (*salma* or *salmata*), a standardized horse-load, while a *muid* (*modius*) was a standardized cart-load, equal to 5 or 6 seams.

Setier (*sextarium*), a volume measure of grain, equal to 4 quarters or 2 *émines* or 1/12 *muid* or about 156 litres: Zupko, 147, 166.

Tun (*tunella*), 42 cubic feet or 2000 pounds; pipe (*pipa*), about half a tun: Zupko, 137, 176.

Piece (*pecia*), a shipping-barrel of wine, sometimes a pipe: Zupko, 133.

Linear measures occur in these accounts only for cloth:

Brasse (*bracia*), about 1.6 m.: Zupko, 30.
Canne (*canna*), equal to 8 pans (*palme*) or about 2 meters: Zupko, 33, 126.
Ell (*alna*), about 1.2 meters: Zupko, 11.

1. The Life and Family of Pierre de Cros

A. Ecclesiastical Career

The epitaph of Pierre de Cros, engraved in bronze in the college priory of S. Martial in Avignon, summarized his life in the conventional way, as a course of ecclesiastical honors:[1]

> Hic iacet bone memorie reverendissimus in Christo pater dominus Petrus de Croso, oriundus de Calma-forti Lemovicensis diocesis, decretorum doctor; qui primo fuit monachus S. Martialis Lemovicensis ordinis S. Benedicti, et inde prepositus de Rossaco dictorum ordinis et diocesis, postmodum cellerarius ecclesie Tutellensis, et post prior de Volta ordinis Cluniacensis S. Flori diocesis, et deinde abbas regularis monasterii Trenorchiensis Cabilonensis diocesis, et post episcopus S. Papuli; postmodum archiepiscopus Bituricensis, et existente archiepiscopo fuit factus camerarius domini nostri pape per sancte memorie dominum Gregorium papam XI et deinde archiepiscopum Arelatensem; et de ecclesia Arelatensi et camerariatu predictis fuit assumtus in tituli SS. Nerei et Achillei presbyterum cardinalem, qui sanitate fungens hic suam elegit sepulturam. Orate Deum pro anima ipsius universi et singuli huc convenientes suum tumulum inspecturi.

The written records shed further light on the epitaph and permit us to gloss it line by line.[2] Pierre de Cros was born about 1322, as a later document will show. His birthplace and that of his brother Jean, the château called *Calma fortis* in Latin, is Lachaud, now a hamlet of about fifty residents, midway between Le Puy-en-Velay and Brioude by national route 102, overlooking the Fioule, one of the high tributaries of the Allier. Pierre de Cros named in his testament the parish in which he was baptized: S. Exupéry-les-Roches (department of Corrèze, canton and arrondissement of Ussel). There is also a hamlet named Cros 7.4 km southeast of S. Exupéry. Delphine de Cros was designated lady of *Calma* in an instrument of 22 August 1342 establishing a perpetual vicar in S. Exupéry for the altar or chapel of *Calma*. Both Pierre's parents were buried at S. Exupéry, and

---

[1] *GC* 1: 579D–580A.

[2] Outline in Ulysse Chevalier, *Répertoire des sources historiques du moyen âge: Biobibliographie* 1 (Paris, 1905), 1075–76; a better sketch by Guillaume Mollat in *DHGE* 13 (1956): 1066, amplified by Michel Hayez in *Lexikon des Mittelalters* 3:356–57.

Delphine was probably his mother.[3] In any case, Pierre de Cros belonged by birth and baptism to the diocese of Limoges, although his parish was 100 kilometers distant from the cathedral city.

Other than this epitaph, I have seen no hint that Pierre de Cros was a doctor of Canon law. The university dignity was certainly not noted in connection with any of his prelatial appointments, although the papal bulls on such occasions always mentioned whatever justifications might exist for such an elevation in rank. No university, college, or professor is remembered in Pierre's testaments. His doctorate might have been of the spontaneous, quasi-honorary sort once distributed by his distant cousin Guillaume d'Aigrefeuille the younger, on the very day when he became a doctor himself, to nine of his colleagues at Toulouse.[4] In any case, Pierre de Cros was probably too young to be *decretorum doctor* before his profession in the Benedictine order, as the sequence of achievements in the epitaph seems to suggest.

Pierre made his permanent profession as a Benedictine monk in the abbey of S. Martial de Limoges, and then began rising within the order. To begin, he took up two offices when Raimond d'Aigrefeuille, an early beneficiary of the Limousin papacy, resigned them. Pierre appears as provost of Roussac (Limoges) in a document of 6 July 1342.[5] Then, on 5 February 1343, his appointment as cellarer of the cathedral priory of Tulle was approved, with a dispensation for his deficiency of age: he was in his twentieth year "vel circiter."[6] Next he was prior of La Voûte-Chillac OClun (S. Flour), probably needing a papal permission to change from Benedictine to Cluniac before he could take up the benefice.

Pierre became abbot of Tournus OSB (Chalon-sur-Saône) on 20 February 1348. The bull of appointment to this reserved abbacy mentions no blood relation to Clement VI, but it does declare that Pierre was "in sacerdotio constitutum, apud nos de litterarum scientia, religionis zelo, honestate morum, vite munditia, spiritualium et temporalium providentia, aliisque donis virtutum, fidedignorum testimoniis multiplicibus commendatum." In a mildly humorous allusion to his shifts from order to order, the bull noted that Pierre would have to wear the Benedictine habit at Tournus even though he was himself a Cluniac

---

[3] Baluze-Mollat 3:819; Michel Hayez in *Lexikon des Mittelalters* 3:355. Two tombstones in the church, carved with the arms of de Cros and Roger, are shown by Pierrette and Robert Merceron and Hervé Aliquot, "Armorial des cardinaux limousins de la papauté d'Avignon," *Lemouzi* 60 (1980): 399–411, here 400.

[4] Baluze-Mollat 1:408. Five Aigrefeuille brothers, favored by their cousin Clement VI, became prelates, and Guillaume d'Aigrefeuille was the son of the only one who remained a layman: Bernard Guillemain, *La Cour pontificale d'Avignon (1309-1376): Etude d'une société*, 2d ed. (Paris, 1966), 270. For Faydit d'Aigrefeuille see Robert Gane, *Le chapitre de Notre-Dame de Paris au XIVe s.* (Saint-Etienne, 1999), 271–72, no. 5.

[5] Albanès 3: *Arles*, 710, no. 1641.

[6] Albanès 3: *Arles*, 710, no. 1642.

monk. He was permitted by another bull to receive his blessing as abbot from a bishop of his own choice.[7]

He entered the secular hierarchy as bishop of S. Papoul, confirmed by Innocent VI and obligated for his services on 27 July 1362.[8] De Cros' first work in service to the Camera Apostolica soon followed. He was commissioned by the chamberlain Arnaud Aubert, another son of the Limousin, to farm out the income of the priory of Ispagnac (Mende) in 1364. The farm or rent was to be spent on the fortification of Ispagnac, which guarded a bridge on the upper Tarn, the works being supervised by the knight Garin Garin, lord of Tournel.[9] The business did not go well: Calendar no. 166 is its tangled record. On one occasion Pierre spoke for his colleagues, the bishops of the province, protesting that the archbishop of Toulouse was arrogating jurisdiction over them.[10] Still, he joined those colleagues in a letter patent of 1369 by which they promulgated the indulgences for visiting the tomb of S. Thomas Aquinas in the Dominican convent of Toulouse.[11]

Urban V, in one of his last official acts at Montefiascone before the long vacation of his Curia and its return to Avignon, promoted Pierre d'Estaing, archbishop of Bourges, to the rank of cardinal, replacing him in Bourges with Pierre de Cros.[12] The pope was providing for an uncertain future, creating a strong cardinal legate for Italy and preparing a successor for his ailing chamberlain Arnaud Aubert.[13] He was probably relying on the advice of Cardinal Guillaume

---

[7] Albanès 3: *Arles*, 710–11, nos. 1643 and 1644.

[8] Albanès 3: *Arles*, 712, no. 1645.

[9] Garin had sponsored the petition of one Bertrand de Cros, cleric of Mende, for a reservation in December 1362 (Suppliques 36:1024). I have found no indication that Bertrand was related to Pierre de Cros.

[10] EFR *Urbain V communes*, no. 22369. The archbishop was Geoffroi de Veyrols (1361–1377).

[11] Toulouse, Archives départementales de la Haute-Garonne, 112 H 9, no. 26. The letter bears the episcopal seal, described by the Archives repertory: "Au tiers supérieur le Christ en croix, les jambes repliées, entre la Vierge à gauche nimbée et en buste et saint Jean aussi nimbé et en buste. Au-dessous deux saints revêtus d'habits sacerdotaux, à gauche un évêque nimbé, mitré, bénissant de la main droite et tenant une croix; à droite un saint tonsuré, nimbé, tenant une palme de la main droite et un livre sur sa poitrine. Au-dessous l'évêque mitré à genoux, les mains tenant sa crosse accosté de deux blasons: à gauche un écartelé de fleurs de lys et d'une croix de Jérusalem [Aquitaine], à droite un écu vairé [de Cros]."

[12] On 7 and 9 June 1370, respectively: Albanès 3: *Arles*, 712–13, no. 1646. Responding to Italian sensibilities, the pope created one other cardinal at this farewell moment, Pietro Corsini, then bishop of Florence. The vacation of the Curia was to run from the beginning of June to the beginning of October: Baluze-Mollat 1:375.

[13] Aubert Calendar, 22–23.

d'Aigrefeuille and of Arnaud Aubert himself, the major Limousin voices in the Curia in Italy.

The pope landed at Marseille on 17 September 1370. Two days later the cité of Limoges, the cathedral and citadel precinct, was stormed and sacked by troops of the Black Prince.[14] The captains Roger de Beaufort, Jean de la Roche, and Jean de Villemur and the bishop Jean de Cros were among those taken prisoner. When Urban died in December, it is clear that sympathy for the sufferings of Limoges played a significant part in the election of Pierre Roger de Beaufort as Pope Gregory XI. It is also certain that the new pope's policies were deeply influenced by the sack of Limoges. He made the dispossessed bishop, his cousin Jean de Cros, a cardinal at the very earliest opportunity. He gave lavishly to his brother Guillaume de Beaufort, viscount of Turenne, to uphold the military state of their family and of the papal court. He worked strenuously to ransom Roger de Beaufort (also his brother) and Jean de la Roche (his nephew) from their English captors; and he undertook to raise funds for the redemption of castles in the Limousin from the English.

Pierre de Cros, brother of the new cardinal Jean and cousin of the new pope, stepped into a position of great influence in the Curia. As early as 20 February 1371, four months before he was appointed chamberlain, we see him exercising patronage at the highest level and with privileged access to papal power. In the secret book kept by the *referendarius* Pierre Flandrin are noted the benefices which the pope especially reserved for the clients of privileged curialists, Pierre de Cros among them.[15] Later, as chamberlain, de Cros was competent to receive resignations of benefices and, like his predecessors, he acted as a broker for the exchange of benefices.[16] He seems to have used his patronage moderately, favoring the Limousin clergy in general, not only his nearest relatives.

The office of chamberlain proved so absorbing that Pierre never engaged closely with his church of Bourges. This was normal for a curial prelate, to whom an episcopal *mensa* was a normal appanage, the source of a noble income in office. A clash of lay and ecclesiastical interests over some rents and dues was also normal, and Gregory XI had to warn Jean, duc de Berry, not to permit his officers

---

[14] The circumstances are most clearly explained by Henri Denifle, *La désolation des églises, monastères et hôpitaux en France pendant la Guerre de Cent Ans* (Paris, 1899), 2:559–62.

[15] Michel Hayez, "Les réserves spéciales de bénéfices sous Urbain V et Grégoire XI," in *Aux origines de l'état moderne* (Rome, 1990), 237–49, here 239, 242. The secret register, now Archives départementales de Vaucluse, D 204, was kept by successive papal referendarii, each of whom later became cardinal: Pierre Flandrin through 1371; Guy de Malessec until September 1376 when the pope departed from Marseille for Italy; and Martin de Zalva from 5 April 1377 in Rome.

[16] EFR *Grégoire XI communes*, no. 13083.

to infringe the archbishop's rights in Bourges.[17] The pope also asked the king of France to postpone the archbishop's homage for his royal fiefs.[18]

Arles, the major metropolitan see of Provence, became vacant by the translation of archbishop Guillaume de la Garde to the Latin patriarchate of Jerusalem on 12 December 1371. For almost three years the see was kept vacant for the profit of the Camera. Then on 2 August 1374 Pierre de Cros was transferred from Bourges to Arles. He made some gestures toward a pastoral relation, providing for emergency supplies of grain to Salon, a town belonging to his *mensa*, in August 1374, and visiting Arles at Christmas that year.[19] On 7 April 1376, observing the custom of Limousin prelates, he founded a chapel of S. Martial in the cathedral of S. Trophime; and on 7 August 1376, shortly before departing with the pope for Italy, he founded two daily masses in the cathedral, one to the Virgin and one to S. Martial.[20] After the two papal elections of 1378 Urban VI tried to cut the seditious chamberlain off from his income, and at the same time to attract the queen of Naples to his obedience, by deposing Pierre de Cros from Arles and offering the see to a relative of the queen's husband Otto of Brunswick. Queen Joan, firmly loyal to the Limousin ecclesiastical clan which had loyally supported her, refused the offer. Instead she ordered her seneschal of Provence to keep the church's properties safe for Pierre de Cros.[21] Clement VII's Chancery at Anagni, reacting over-cautiously to Urban's gambit, moved Pierre to Toulouse as of 24 January 1379, promoting Jean Flandrin, dean of Laon, to Arles. Pierre, when he learned of his translation, refused it.[22]

---

[17] 17 August 1371, repeated 3 January 1372: EFR *Grégoire XI secrètes France*, nos. 350 and 573. Similar letters were sent to Philip duke of Burgundy, Louis duke of Anjou, Edward prince of Aquitaine and Wales, John duke of Lancaster, and Edmund earl of Cambridge: nos. 574–578.

[18] 9 November 1372: EFR *Grégoire XI secrètes France*, no. 977, citing RV 268, 202r.

[19] EFR *Grégoire XI secrètes autres*, no. 2811; Baluze-Mollat 1:422 for the grain shortage of that year; VQ 6:517. There is a hiatus in the Calendar between 16 December 1374 and 8 January 1375.

[20] Albanès 3: *Arles*, nos. 1655 and 1656, col. 716.

[21] Eubel, ad Arelaten., note: "In aliqua relatione mense Octobris 1378 ab Aegidio Bellemère missa cardinalibus Avinione residentibus legimus inter alia: 'Item Bartholomeus contulit (deposito Petro archiepiscopo) ecclesiam Arelatensem cuidam fratri vel nepoti domini de Brunswick, qui insidiatur latenter castris et fortalitiis dictae ecclesiae, et idcirco provideatur per mandatum reginae dirigendum senescalco, quod protegat et defendat dominum camerarium et volentem occupare impediat et viriliter expellat.'"

[22] Eubel, 1: 488, n. 7 ad Tolosan.: "Jam 1379 Jan. 24 Cle. VII (Av. t. 15 f. 423) Petrum (Cros) aep. Arelaten. ad Tolosan. transtulit, sed haec translatio effectum non habuit." The bull, dated Fondi, is in Albanès 3: *Arles*, no. 1664, cols. 719–20. Clement VII had previously granted Toulouse *in commendam* to the Latin patriarch of Alexandria. Jean Flandrin, who was to have succeeded Pierre de Cros at Arles (*Arles*, no. 1665, cols. 720–21) instead got Auch in May 1379.

He continued his service as chamberlain in the Curia of Clement VII at Avignon until his brother, Cardinal Jean de Cros, died (21 November 1383), and at age sixty Pierre was given a red hat and relieved of his powerful and onerous ministry.

On 23 December 1383 he was created cardinal priest of the title of SS. Nereus and Achilleus, which had once been his brother's title. He was called the cardinal of Arles, and he continued to administer the church of Arles, that is, to collect its income, until his death. He also continued to serve his family and regional interests, as executor of the testament of his brother and in 1384 administering a long-delayed bequest of Cardinal Hugues Roger.[23] He had taken up residence in his brother's house, the livrée de Mirault near the papal palace,[24] and it was there that he dictated his two testaments and there that he died on 16 November 1388.

B. Family Connections

Bernard Guillemain, assiduous detective of the papal court at Avignon, has pointed out that from 1342 to 1378 twenty-seven cardinals were created who came from the Limousin, although earlier and later that country was seldom so favored.[25] It was the generation of three Limousin popes, two Limousin papal chamberlains, three Limousin chamberlains of the College of Cardinals, and one tenacious Limousin vice-chancellor, all of them served by households and staffs who were mostly Limousins. These well-placed ecclesiastics and their clans relished the glory of their three papacies, stubbornly resisted the transplantation of the Curia back to Italy, fostered their own and each others' family estates in the Church and under the French crown, intermarried intricately and called each other "cousin" on the basis of relations which we can no longer trace. Pierre de Cros, for example, addressed Bernard de Bonval, bishop of Bologna, and Gerald du Puy, abbot of Marmoutiers, "Reverendi patres et consanguinei carissimi" in a letter (Calendar no. 74) directing their efforts to bring order to the Italian estates of the Church. In short, they considered themselves a proud national community, one of the legitimate constituent elements of the Curia and hierarchy, just as the *nationes* or *linguae* were constituents of the major universities of Paris, Bologna, and Toulouse.

---

[23] J. Becquet, "La fondation du chapitre S.-Germain près Masseret par le cardinal de Tulle (XIV siècle)," *Lemouzi* 65 (1985): 239–43.

[24] The liveries of Avignon are topographically and historically described by Anne-Marie Hayez, "Les livrées avignonnaises de la période pontificale," *Mémoires de l'Académie de Vaucluse*, 8e série, 1 (1992): 93–130; 2 (1993): 15–57; 3 (1994): 33–89. For the livrée de Mirault, see 1 (1992): 109, nos. 96–98.

[25] Guillemain, *La Cour*, 183–89.

We can be quite sure of their opinions and intentions regarding their home country, their community, and the Church. The founding father of the Limousin clan in the Curia, Pierre Roger, was tellingly quoted by a fifteenth-century Norman chronicler.[26] Newly crowned as Pope Clement VI, gesturing toward his family coat of arms, six red roses *en orle* above and below a band, he said, "I will plant in the Church such a rosebush of this folk and nation of the Limousin that in a hundred years there will be no corner without its roots and rosebuds." The anonymous memory may have been colored by subsequent events and by discontent with an archbishop of Rouen who did so little for Normandy. But well before he was elected pope, Pierre Roger had already begun the building of his extended family, nation, and party into a single political force, in collaboration with Etienne Aubert, later Pope Innocent VI.

At the Michaelmas Court of King Philip VI at S. Christophe-en-Halatte in 1338, Etienne Aubert made his entry with a noble entourage of a hundred and thirty-three men all in coats of his arms (three scallops above a lion, barred), new couture of Toulouse.[27] The display of livery was in keeping with his rank as bishop of Noyon and peer of France, king's counsel in the Parlement de Paris; but it was far beyond Aubert's resources as head of a small, recently noble and not yet rich Limousin family. For the occasion he had enlisted all his own family and official staffs and squires, some mere boys, also several body-servants and even his barber, and there were four anonymous couriers kindly lent to swell his progress by Cardinal Talleyrand of Périgord. A good number in the parade, however, were members of the near and extended Roger family, and these were such men as did not have to be hidden in the rear, for example the heir of the count of Beaufort and the future Pope Gregory XI, eight years old at the time. A Limousin alliance was at work, a political constellation beginning to form around the mutual favor and loyalty of the two bishops who were also heads of their families. The flag of this new party, planted in dedicated chapels and colleges by successful Limousin prelates one after another, was the cult of S. Martial of Limoges.

S. Martial's Life was written early in the eleventh century by Adhémar de Chabannes, who attributed it to a first-century Aurelianus. The ancient monastery of Limoges dedicated in his name treasured this pious forgery, according to which S. Martial was not only the "apostle of the Limousin" in a general sense, an early preacher of the Gospel and founder of churches there, but much more: a convert to the preaching of Jesus, closely associated with the twelve apostles and especially with Peter, a kinsman.[28] In the 1330s the Dominican historian and

---

[26] Baluze-Mollat 2:578, citing BNF, MS. fr. 5391, fol. 37r.

[27] Daniel Williman, "Memoranda and Sermons of Etienne Aubert (Innocent VI) as Bishop (1338–1341)," *Mediaeval Studies* 37 (1975): 7–41.

[28] Walter de Grey Birch, ed., "*Vita Sanctissimi Martialis Apostoli*: The Life of St. Martial by Aurelianus, from a Manuscript in the British Museum," *Journal of the British Archaeological Association* 28 (1872): 353–90. A French version of the 13th century is

inquisitor Bernard Gui added the Limoges legend of Martial to his own studies of the Seventy-two Disciples and of the saints and bishops of Aquitaine, lending his considerable scholarly authority to the legend.[29] Shortly after his consecration as pope in 1342 Clement VI issued a bull authorizing the celebration of S. Martial's day, 30 June, with the vigil and mass appropriate to an apostle.[30] Two years later the pope's court painter Matteo Giovanetti put the legend in fresco on the walls and ceiling of the S. Martial Chapel in the palace at Avignon.[31] This chapel was entered only from the Grand Tinel, the Curia's dining hall, and the painted scenes were clearly designed for glory and propaganda: they are marked with capital letters, to be pointed out in the proper sequence. Here we can still see the essential scenes of the fictive Martial's life, among his fellow apostles and later in Limoges, and here are ranged, with their names, the many cathedral churches which were credited to him as founder. One painted scene is an audacious supplement to the Adhémar-Gui legend: Jesus places his hand on the boy Martial's head, and the book open before him reads "NISI": it must be Matthew 18:3, "Unless you become like little ones you shall not enter the kingdom of heaven." Among the many portraits in this charming chapel, it could be that we have here the face and form of Clement VI's nephew, the fourteen-year-old Limousin courtier Pierre Roger de Beaufort, the future Pope Gregory XI.

The business and the fortunes of the papal court through the early career of Pierre de Cros were interwoven with those of the Roger and Aubert clans. Arnaud Aubert had gained and implemented the office of papal chamberlain in harmony with family interests, and his successor Pierre de Cros followed suit, bringing his family into profitable relations with the Curia and developing his own authority and fortune by his relation, his loyalty, and his service to his Roger cousinage.

The precise link between Roger and Cros, however, has disappeared. I cannot be sure of the name of the Roger lady who was the daughter of Guillaume, lord of Rosiers d'Egletons and the sister of Clement VI,[32] nor the name of the noble de Cros whom she married, but she was the mother of the elder cardinal Pierre de Cros and the grandmother of three de Cros churchmen including the younger Pierre, our papal chamberlain. For the elder Pierre de Cros was Clement

---

Wauchier de Denain, *La Vie Seint Marcel de Lymoges*, ed. Molly Lynde-Recchia (Geneva, 2005). The *Acta Sanctorum* ignores this legend.

[29] Toulouse, Bibliothèque municipale, MS. 477 is a collection of saints' lives, including Adhémar's life of S. Martial, assembled for Bernard Gui.

[30] The bull *Piam sanctorum memoriam* of 5 July 1343: ASV RV 215, 6v-7r.

[31] Splendidly revealed by Dominique Vingtain, *Avignon: Le Palais des Papes*, with photographs by Claude Sauvageot (n.p., 1998), 290–342 and color plates nos. 56–82.

[32] This could possibly be Almodie Roger, sister of Clement VI, only if she was left widowed by the death of a de Cros husband before being proposed in 1342 for marriage to Guillaume de Besse. That marriage was apparently never solemnized, *pace* Baluze-Mollat 2:382; instead, Jacques de Besse linked those families by marrying Delphine Roger.

VI's nephew, according to the act of the Consistory where he was created cardinal, and the younger one's brother Jean was "a cousin of Pope Gregory XI in the third degree."[33] This means that "either Jean's [and Pierre's] grandmother was a Roger, or Gregory's grandmother was of the family de Cros."[34] But Gregory's father's mother, we know, was Guillemette de Mestre, and if Gregory's mother's mother had been de Cros, Clement VI would have been related to the family de Cros only by his brother's marriage, not by blood.

All the de Cros prelates displayed the same family arms without difference. These are unusual, and there has been no consensus as to their color or content. The head of the shield might be plain or cut off, and the remainder has been considered to represent *vair* (stylized squirrel-fur); or three decks of dovecote with 3, 2 and 1 square pigeonholes; or three panels of battlement with 3, 2 and 1 merlons.[35] A ceremonial sword of Pierre de Cros, now in a private collection in France, seems to settle the question. The somewhat crudely enameled shield on the pommel has four rows of red merlons on a field of gold (red enamel filling the spaces carved out of the latten or brass plaque on the sword's pommel). The *chef* is cut off by two red lines and contains two ranges of "achievements" separated by another red line: above, three blue pyramid shapes and below, one truncated blue pyramid. The other face of the pommel has a golden ARCH/IEPISC/OPUS + outlined in red champlevé.[36]

---

[33] Baluze-Mollat 1:417. The degrees of relation are clearly explained by A. W. Renton and G. G. Phillimore, *The Comparative Law of Marriage and Divorce* (London, 1910), 21: "The civil law, in reckoning degrees, counts, as regards the direct line, a degree for each generation; as regards collaterals, it counts from one of the persons whose relationship is in question up to the common ancestor, and then down to the other. The canon law reckoned direct relationship in the same way, but in the collateral line it counted only up to the common ancestor, and not down again. According to this mode of computation first cousins are in the second degree, because each of them is only two generations distant from the common stock. In the unequal collateral line, where one of the two is further removed than the other from the common ancestor, the canon law reckons the distance by the number of generations of the person furthest removed." In this case the common stock is Guillaume, lord of Rosiers d'Egleton.

[34] Baluze-Mollat 2:336.

[35] The blazons are shown and described in Merceron and Aliquot, "Armorial des cardinaux limousins," 399–411; cf. Max Prinet, "Les armoiries de Pierre de Cros, archevêque de Bourges," *Mémoires de la Société des antiquaires du Centre* 38 (1917–1918): 59–62.

[36] My thanks to Peter Finer for the photographs, which may be found on the compact disk enclosed with this book; a full description of the sword appears in his catalogue of military antiquities for 2003.

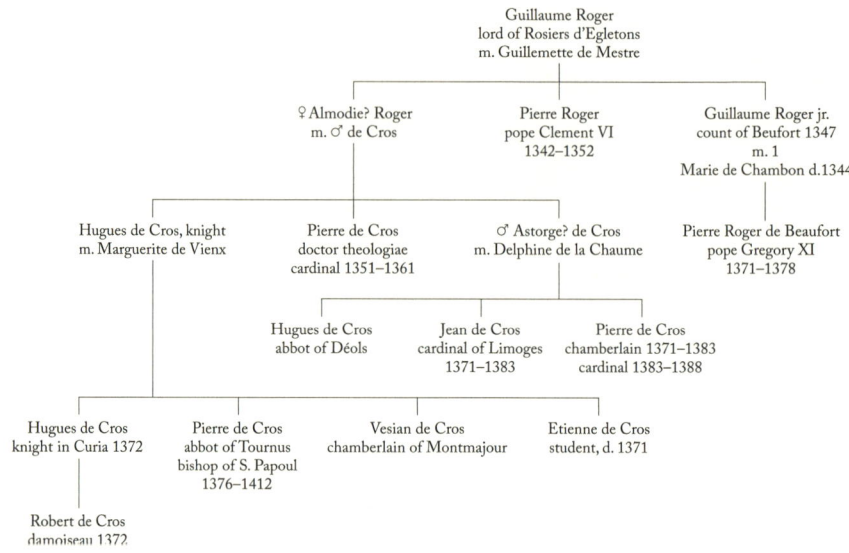

FIGURE I.I
Select Genealogy: De Cros and Roger.

The elder Cardinal Pierre de Cros[37] was nephew and protegé of Clement VI (Pierre Roger). Professed Benedictine and fellow of the Sorbonne, he was master of arts, bachelor of theology (1335), licentiate in theology (1337), doctor of theology (1338), and provisor of the Sorbonne (1340), following Pierre Roger in that office. He attended the household of Etienne Aubert at S. Christophe in 1338.[38] In 1344, when Pierre de Cros was already dean of Paris, Clement VI promoted him to bishop of Senlis, then transferred him to Auxerre in 1349. The pope presented his nephew to the Consistory of December 1350 and created him cardinal, giving him the title of S. Martinus in Montibus when he appeared in the Curia in April 1351. He died of the plague at Avignon in 1361, leaving many benefices vacant: he had been canon of Bourges; archdeacon of Châteauroux (Bourges); archdeacon of Lieuvin (Lisieux); archdeacon of Beaugency (Orléans); provost of S. Willehard, Bremen; canon of the cathedral and of Xanten (Cologne) and treasurer of S. Severin, Cologne; archpriest of Cazouls (Béziers).[39]

---

[37] Biography by Michel Hayez in *Lexikon des Mittelalters* 3:355; and see Gane, *Chapitre de Notre-Dame*, 308–9, no. 194.

[38] Williman, "Memoranda," 14, no. A 30.

[39] EFR *Urbain V communes*, nos. 1996, 2271, 4732, 4804, 9585, 11638, 13385; Suppliques 36, 396; 37, 332, 940 and 941; 38, 570, 707 and 1686; 39, 1663; 42, 1884.

The rest of the Cros family tree must be drawn by means of occasional hints, since there is no contemporary genealogy. Two brothers of the first Cardinal Pierre de Cros seem to have married: Hugues to Marguerite de Vienx, and the other, possibly named Astorge,[40] to Delphine de la Chaume; these were the parents of Cardinal Jean de Cros, of our Pierre de Cros, and of Abbot Hugues de Cros of Déols.

Jean de Cros, the elder brother of our Pierre, began his career as a student of civil law at Orléans.[41] Benedict XII gave him a canonry with prebend of Limoges (22 June 1339), and somewhat later he became canon of Paris for life. Doctor of laws and prior of the secular church of Vatan (Indre), he was confirmed as bishop of Limoges on 14 May 1347. He was bishop of Limoges at the time of the sack, September 1370, captured by the English, and redeemed by Charles V of France for 100 francs in February 1371. The pope created him cardinal priest of the title of SS. Nereus and Achilleus on 30 May 1371. As cardinal, Jean de Cros engaged in the brokerage of benefices in the papal court, receiving resignations, assembling *permutationes* (multiple simultaneous exchanges), and endorsing supplications.[42] He had the informal title of cardinal of Limoges; he was cardinal penitentiary from 21 October 1373; and he was promoted cardinal bishop of Palestrina on 24 September 1376. Mistrusted and harshly treated by Urban VI, Jean de Cros was one of the ambassadors to France who urged the Clementist cause at Vincennes on 7 May 1379, and on 16 August 1379 he rejoined the Curia which had reassembled at Avignon. His death on 21 or 22 November 1383 was the occasion for Clement VII to promote his brother Pierre de Cros from chamberlain to cardinal, with Jean's old title of SS. Nereus and Achilleus. Jean de Cros was buried in the cathedral of Avignon, Notre Dame des Doms, near his first benefactor Benedict XII.

The official career of Pierre de Cros the younger has already been described.

Hugues de Cros, a younger brother, imitated Pierre's early career by occupying posts of financial responsibility in the monastic order. He was chamberlain of Clairac OSB (Agen);[43] then almoner of Déols OSB (Bourges), and abbot there

---

[40] Among the lay members of Etienne Aubert's household in 1338 we find "Asturgono nepoti domini Rothomagensis," i.e., nephew of Pierre Roger, archbishop of Rouen, later Clement VI: Williman, "Memoranda," 15, no. A 61.

[41] Guillaume Mollat, "Cros (Jean de)," *DHGE* 13 (1956), cols. 1064–65; Michel Hayez, "Cros Jean de, Kard.," *Lexikon des Mittelalters* 3:355; Gane, *Chapitre de Notre-Dame*, 308, no. 193.

[42] EFR *Grégoire XI communes*, nos. 6108, 6109, 9441, 9442. Jean and Pierre de Cros were two of a very few officials permitted by the pope to receive resignations of benefices when these were intended for exchange by their holders; see Anne-Marie Hayez, "Un aperçu de la politique bénéficiale de Grégoire XI," in *Forschungen zur Reichs-, Papst- und Landesgeschichte* (Stuttgart, 1998), 2: 685–98, here 690.

[43] EFR *Urbain V communes*, no. 18963.

by 1372, until his death in 1384.[44] Pierre de Cros as chamberlain overrode his brother's plea, that he could not pay 2000 florins for his services and procurations, by seizing the revenues of Châteauponsac, a property of the abbey in Limoges diocese (Calendar no. 170). Part of Hugues' spoils were allowed to revert to his mother Delphine de Cros.[45]

The surname de Cros appears frequently in the records of the Curia in the 1370s, and a few relatives of Pierre de Cros can be picked out with a fair degree of confidence. He and his brother the cardinal were useful patrons to a handful of first cousins, sons of an uncle of theirs. This second married brother of the first Cardinal Pierre de Cros may well have been the knight Hugues de Cros of Limoges diocese whose widow, Marguerite de Vienx, got an indulgence for absolution *in articulo mortis* in 1372.[46] I surmise that they were the parents of another Hugues de Cros, knight in the Curia of Gregory XI, who received a free pass as escort for 24 barrels of wine to the palace on 18 September 1372,[47] and who might (by a further surmise) be the father of Robert de Cros, damoiseau of Limoges diocese, who received a winter clothing allowance in the Curia, together with another papal cousin Raoul de Lestranges, on 11 March 1372.[48] In the supposititious family tree, I have also allocated as sons of the elder knight Hugues de Cros (first cousins of our Pierre de Cros) two monks and a student:

Etienne de Cros, as a scholar of civil law at Toulouse in June 1371, was granted a canonry of Albi and the secular priory *sine cura* of S. Pierre-de-Cardeilhac (S. Bertrand-de-Comminges); later the same year he resigned the canonry but not the priory into the hands of Hugues, bishop of Albi, in exchange for a second sinecure priory, that of S. Jean-de-la-Buade (Béziers). By *motu proprio* of Gregory XI on 7 October 1372 he was granted the office of provost *sine cura* of Eymoutiers (Limoges); here he was noted as a student of canon law at Toulouse and *germanus* (here meaning first cousin) of Cardinal Jean de Cros. It was this cardinal who arranged in June 1373, after Etienne's death, to transfer the priory of Cardeilhac to another of his relatives, Hugues de Bonfont; the priory of La Buade went to another student canonist of Toulouse, and Eymoutiers to yet another.[49]

Pierre de Cros, bachelor of canon law, Benedictine monk, and chamberlain of the cathedral monastery of S. Papoul, was granted the priory of Labruguière

---

[44] In 1372 he received an indulgence for absolution *in articulo mortis*: EFR *Grégoire XI communes*, no. 17287.

[45] Daniel Williman, *The Right of Spoil of the Popes of Avignon 1316–1415* (Philadelphia, 1988), 145, no. 550.

[46] EFR *Grégoire XI communes*, no. 17288.

[47] VQ 6:688.

[48] VQ 6:388.

[49] EFR *Grégoire XI communes*, nos. 11069, 13044, 19445, 25201, 25204.

OSB (Lavaur) on 9 January 1371.[50] He was probably first cousin of our chamberlain and followed closely in his footsteps. He is noted as abbot of Tournus in 1375, then as bishop of S. Papoul from 18 August 1376; he died in 1412.[51]

Vesian de Cros, chamberlain of S. Victor de Marseille, could possibly be an elder brother of Etienne and Pierre.[52] As chamberlain of Montmajour he transferred to the abbot, who was equipping a galley, a payment from the papal treasure, 7 August 1369.[53] There is a select, annotated tree of the extended Roger-Beaufort family below.

C. Testaments and Succession of Pierre de Cros

Pierre de Cros died on 16 November 1388, almost five years after leaving office as chamberlain. He dictated two testaments in the last year of his life. Baluze edited both from originals in the archives of the Collège de S. Martial, Avignon.[54]

The first testament, of 27 February 1388, enacted in the secret or retreat chamber of the cardinal's house in Avignon, was less carefully prepared and more discursive than the later one. In the first version, de Cros named as his universal heirs whomever of Christ's poor his executors might choose. He named five executors: Cardinals Gui de Malessec (Palestrina) and Pierre de Sortenac (Sabina), and his own chaplains Jean Sabatier, *decretorum doctor*, sacristan of Agde (his auditor); Geraud Mercadier, provost of Vence, his chamberlain; and Simon le Fay, canon of Bourges. The last three also witnessed the testament.

Relying upon a testamentary license granted by Clement VII,[55] Pierre de Cros commended his soul and body to the Creator, the Virgin Mary, and Saints Michael, John the Baptist, Martial, Benedict, and Nereus and Achilleus. He chose to be buried in monk's habit, with a cross of red on black cloth on his chest, either in the tomb of his brother Cardinal Jean de Cros in the cathedral church

---

[50] EFR *Grégoire XI communes*, nos. 5308, 5312, 15022.

[51] Chevalier, *Bio-bibliographie*, 1:1075. This younger Pierre de Cros was elected by the chapter of S. Papoul, then confirmed by Gregory XI, 18 August 1376: Albanès 3: *Arles*, no. 1657, col. 716.

[52] EFR *Urbain V communes*, no. 16196; Suppliques 45, 842.

[53] VQ 6:276.

[54] Baluze-Mollat 4:318–27. The testaments are found today in the S. Martial necrology, Avignon, BM, MS. 2466, fols. 131rv and 135rv.

[55] As bishop of S. Papoul he had a license dated 22 February 1363: EFR *Urbain V communes*, no. 5753. Thierry Soulard, "Un inventaire d'orfèvrerie du 14e siècle: l'exécution testamentaire des cardinaux limousins Pierre et Jean de Cros," *Bulletin de la Société archéologique et historique du Limousin* 115 (1988): 32–67, here 53 no. 6 cites without date RV 295, 31r and RV 297, 31v for the licenses of Clement VII to Pierre de Cros.

of Notre-Dame des Doms (with a gift of 50 current florins to the chapter), or in the Cluniac college college priory of S. Martial, Avignon. A hundred paupers were to be given black tunics to carry torches at his funeral. The convents and churches of the city should receive two florins each for attending, the four principal hospitals and the leprosarium outside Porte S. Lazare four florins, and the other hospitals two florins, but the hospital of Salon (Arles) would receive ten florins: all to buy food and clothing for the poor. To each of the women's monastic convents of Avignon, as well as S. Veran and S. Praxed, two florins, but ten to the Soeurs Repenties, the convent of reformed prostitutes, and ten more to their church of Notre-Dame des Miracles.[56]

He left 400 florins in lieu of a "chapel" (a suit of vestments in one color) which he had proposed to give to the chapter of his old church of S. Flour, in return for an anniversary mass. To the abbey of Tournus OSB, his indigo chapel and second-best silver thurible. Of his many books, those with their owners' names written in the back in the hand of d. Guillaume Saxi, priest of Limoges, should be restored to the owners, and the rest sold. To Bourges, his first metropolitan church, he left 400 fl. for an anniversary mass. To Tulle, his white chapel embroidered with birds. To his baptismal church of S. Exupéry (Limoges), a white, an indigo, and a black chasuble for the chapel of the Virgin where his parents were buried, also a silver chalice weighing three marks, a reliquary, and a missal. A thousand florins were to be spent on his funeral, including the vigil customary for a cardinal and black garb for his familiars. He provided for his servants their pay up to the date of his death, with a further year's stipend as bonus. He wished all his silver plate to be sold immediately after his death to pay his debts.

The second testament was dated 13 November 1388, three days before the cardinal died. This one includes a declaration in faith for Clement VII as the true pope. The full payment of his debts was his first provision. His burial now was definitely to be in the college priory of SS. Martial and Benedict. A chapel of S. Stephen there was to be finished for 1300 florins. Two chaplains, monks from the Limousin to be chosen by the abbot of Cluny, were to serve in his funeral chapel by turns, offering a daily mass for the souls of Clement VI, Gregory XI, and Cardinal Jean de Cros; their stipend was to be 20 florins each per year, for their clothing. A house which he had already bought nearby was to be fur-

---

[56] The pope had charged Pierre de Cros in 1373 to gather an endowment for this church (EFR *Grégoire XI secrètes France*, no. 1430), and had ordered him and the bishop of Avignon to direct all unspecified pious bequests to the Repenties (Albanès 7: *Avignon*, no. 1539, 27 October 1374). Gregory XI had transferred from the Pinhota to the Repenties an orchard alongside their church of N.-D. des Miracles on 27 July 1376, just before departing for Italy; it had probably been abandoned by the Pinhota since 1364: Paul Pansier, "L'aumône de la Pignote," *Annuaire de la Société des amis du Palais des Papes et des monuments d'Avignon* 23 (1934): 42–61, here 51; Coll. 51, 369r-372v.

nished as a hospital for Limousin paupers, under the same corporate identity as the priory college church, his new universal heir.[57] Another house, once owned by Raimond de Codolet, was to provide rental income, and all the cardinal's beds and bed-furnishings were donated to the hospital. All these provisions were submitted to the pope's approval and modification. The cardinal ratified in advance certain codicils which he intended to add but which are not known to exist.

The clause designating executors is missing from the transcription of Baluze, but there is a larger list of witnesses here than for the first testament: Pierre de Vernols, bishop of Maguelonne and papal treasurer; Pierre Gérard, bishop of Le Puy; Jean Sabatier, the cardinal's auditor; Geraud Mercadier, his chamberlain; Geraud la Roche OP, papal minor penitentiary; Raimond Rabasse prior of Tornac (Nîmes) and Hugues Tornatoris prior "de Benteriis" (Die); also m. Jean Choat, scribe of the Penitentiary, and the cardinal's chamber servants Guillaume Bertin and Pierre Balène.

There was a strong tradition that cardinals who died in good standing were not subject to the "right of spoil," but the new chamberlain, François de Conzié, must have considered Pierre de Cros a special case, since he died in possession of great personal wealth derived from his ecclesiastical offices, including that of chamberlain. On 28 February 1389 the Camera, arguing the necessities of the war in defense of the Comtat Venaissin against Raimond de Turenne (Pierre de Cros' cousin, as we have seen), formally borrowed from his executors the proceeds of an immense treasure in plate and jewels which Pierre and his brother Jean de Cros had amassed. The estimated value was 11,457 current florins (worth 9734 Cameral florins), from which Catalan de la Roche, the changer of Avignon who advanced the money, took a fee of 100 florins for his trouble in estimating the treasure, and 400 florins more as discounted interest.[58] I have seen no indication that the loan was ever repaid by the Camera or ever demanded by the executors. About one third of those precious goods had belonged to Jean de Cros, two-thirds to Pierre. Pierre's benefices, which now again became a fiscal resource of the Camera, were valued at more than 15,000 florins per year.[59]

---

[57] Recognized in the necrology of S. Martial, where his death and burial are both noted on 17 November 1388: Avignon, BM, MS. 2466, 112rb and 115ra. The priory church, now a Protestant chapel, is entered from rue Henri Fabre by a corridor of two ogival bays whose keystones bear the de Cros arms with cardinal's hat.

[58] The inventory was edited from Coll. 481 and 482 and IM 3375 by Soulard, "Un inventaire d'orfèvrerie," 52–67. Soulard was less than perfectly informed on some technical points, however; like Marc Dykmans, "La fin du séjour des papes en Avignon d'après quelques documents inédits sur les habitations," *Memoires de l'Academie de Vaucluse*, 7e série, 4 (1983): 17–53, here 32 and n. 40, he supposed that the Camera was taking spoils rather than a loan.

[59] Michel Hayez in *Lexikon des Mittelalters* 3:357.

Pierre de Cros was buried according to his choice in the college priory of S. Martial in Avignon, and it was there that his bronze biography was read by the antiquaries cited at the beginning of this chapter.

2. Administration of the Camera Apostolica 1371–1378

From his predecessor, Arnaud Aubert, the chamberlain Pierre de Cros took over a Camera Apostolica that was well organized and staffed by experienced officers and agents, fully capable of financing an energetic papal sovereignty, even in wartime. How well did de Cros manage this fiscal machine? Bernard Guillemain is certainly correct in his judgement that in the appointment of a chamberlain the pope's personal esteem counted more than the candidate's demonstrated financial talent.[1] Pierre de Cros' ablest modern critic, Jean Favier, describing his later activity under Clement VII of Avignon, observes that "the attitude of Pierre de Cros was that of a political man, not an officer narrowly limited to his financial duties. It is absolutely probable that his sights were set higher. His entire bearing betrays the desire for power and the need for action. Evidence enough is provided by his evident lack of interest in the modest affairs of the Camera. He directed these from high above, disdaining to occupy himself with individual cases."[2] The pattern was set in the pontificate of Gregory XI. In this chapter the Cameral administration of those years, and the function of the chamberlain as head of a department of government, will be described in some detail. In the next chapter we will see the larger policies on which he used the discretionary powers of his office and the confidence of the pope, acting as a minister of state.

A. The Chamberlain as Judge

1. *Apostolice Camere*

Pierre de Cros was named *camerarius apostolicus* on 20 June 1371, nine days after the death of his predecessor, Arnaud Aubert. As we have seen, he was the groomed successor and his appointment was no surprise within the Curia. In fact, de Cros had already taken up some functions of the office in the first months of Gregory XI: it was Arnaud Aubert who attended the opening and inventory

---

[1] Guillemain, *La Cour*, 279.
[2] Jean Favier, *Les finances pontificales à l'epoque du Grand Schisme d'Occident (1378–1409)* (Paris, 1966), 42.

of the Upper Treasure on 27 January 1371, but Pierre de Cros was there in his place when the survey continued five days later.[3] Cristoforo da Piacenza, proctor of Mantua at Avignon, whose dispatches are so highly valued for the insights they provide into the activities and gossip of the papal court, made a misleading report on this point in his earliest known letter, dated 20 July 1371.[4] Cristoforo had been remiss in pushing the business of a pardon for the abbot of S. Benedetto di Polirone, excommunicated for non-payment of his common services. He excused himself for the delay, claiming that the abbot's letter of quittance and his release from excommunication could not be obtained, because the chamberlain had died, there were several contenders for the office, and it had not been filled.[5] In truth, Pierre de Cros was busy with his seal of office by 28 June, within a week of his appointment, and he received his full judicial and fiscal powers from Gregory XI on 4 September 1371.

The written commission of the chamberlain, *Apostolice Camere*, begins with an arenga in which the pope premises that the rights and business of the Camera Apostolica are not sufficiently understood by other judges. The chamberlain is therefore empowered to take judicial cognizance of all questions, controversies, causes, and lawsuits, present and future, spiritual, ecclesiastical, and temporal, civil and criminal, those which would have come to the Camera by custom and those which, according to the chamberlain's free decision, concern the Camera directly or indirectly. All persons ecclesiastical and secular, all chapters, colleges, convents, monasteries, and orders, exempt or not, must come to his court when cited (summoned), even if the causes would not customarily be heard at the Apostolic See. The chamberlain may begin such processes, hear them on appeal, or take them away from any other tribunal at any stage. He may delegate these powers. He is permitted to hear these causes "summarily, simply and plainly and without the clamor and formalities of judgement": that is, he may himself determine what is due process, free of the traditional rules. His decisions, whether they be revocations of excommunication, suspension, or interdict, releases, orders, declarations, mandates, decrees, warnings, executory orders, or sentences, are not subject to appeal.

In fact, two bulls dated 4 September 1371, each with the incipit *Apostolice Camere*, were registered for Pierre de Cros, as they had been for his predecessor Arnaud Aubert. The two letters are quite different in their length, their order, and their phrasing, although both versions grant the same large powers.[6] I will

---

[3] Hermann Hoberg, *Die Inventare des päpstlichen Schatzes in Avignon, 1314–1376* (Vatican City, 1944), 486, 496, 509.

[4] Arturo Segrè, ed., "I dispacci di Cristoforo da Piacenza, procuratore mantovano alla corte pontificale (1371–1383)," *Archivio storico italiano*, ser. 5, 43 (1909): 27–95, here 35.

[5] Aubert Calendar, 22–23.

[6] Calendar Appendix B1 and B2, on the compact disk enclosed with this book, are full transcriptions of the two versions.

try to account here for the diplomatic oddity of two simultaneous and equipollent commissions. The doubled commission was a device which Arnaud Aubert had implemented when he was appointed chamberlain in 1361. After seven months in office, Aubert clearly knew what powers he needed to perform the services which he owed to Innocent VI. He experienced no difficulty in getting a grant of those powers from his uncle the pope, under date of 25 October 1361, in the bull *Apostolice Camere per quam incumbentibus*, about 640 words long. Then on 6 December another commission, *Apostolice Camere per quam Sancte*, about 830 words, was issued to him. The two letters were copied, first the one dated later, into an office portfolio of crucial documents that is now part of Collectoriae 359A.

Why did Aubert receive two different letters of commission, and why did his successor de Cros also take both those letters, given that the two texts convey essentially the same powers? The answer seems to lie in a commonplace clause, found in both versions, which insists that the decisions of the chamberlain cannot be reversed "by apostolic letters which do not make a full, express, and verbatim mention of this warrant." The device of two commissions provides a bureaucratic hedge against a formidable potential adversary, one who could get, or who could forge, a papal exemption from the chamberlain's jurisdiction. Such a papal letter, to be effective, would have to incorporate a verbatim recitation of the chamberlain's commission. But whichever text of *Apostolice Camere* might appear in such a privilege, the chamberlain could repel the objection by claiming to be acting under a different commission. In short, it was legitimate authority defended by chicanery. Neither of the successors of Gregory XI engaged in the charade: Urban VI at Rome granted only one letter, the longer one, *Apostolice Camere per quam Sancte*, to his chamberlain Marino dei Giudici, archbishop of Brindisi,[7] and Clement VII at Avignon gave the same letter, with two additional procedural paragraphs, to François de Conzié.[8]

And the chamberlain's commission did not cease with the death of the pope who granted it. Just as Arnaud Aubert had not needed a renewal of *Apostolice Camere* by Urban V or by Gregory XI, but had carried his full authority across two intervals *sede vacante*, Pierre de Cros was known to be the fully empowered chamberlain after Gregory XI died. Using his judicial powers boldly, sitting as apostolic judge in the papal palace of Anagni in the summer of 1378, he gave the cardinals a forum in which to declare their election of Urban VI void and to proceed to the election of Clement VII and the Great Western Schism.[9] Then Clement VII used the services of Pierre de Cros as chamberlain without renewing his commission, because this had never lapsed.

---

[7] *Bullarium Generale* (Lyon, 1655), 291–92, 6 September 1379.

[8] Samaran-Mollat, 247–48, pièces justificatives XXVIII, 24 December 1383.

[9] A full account of de Cros' effort to evict Bartolomeo Prignano from the papacy can be found in Daniel Williman, "Schism within the Curia: The Twin Papal Elections of 1378," *Journal of Ecclesiastical History* 59 (2008): 29–47.

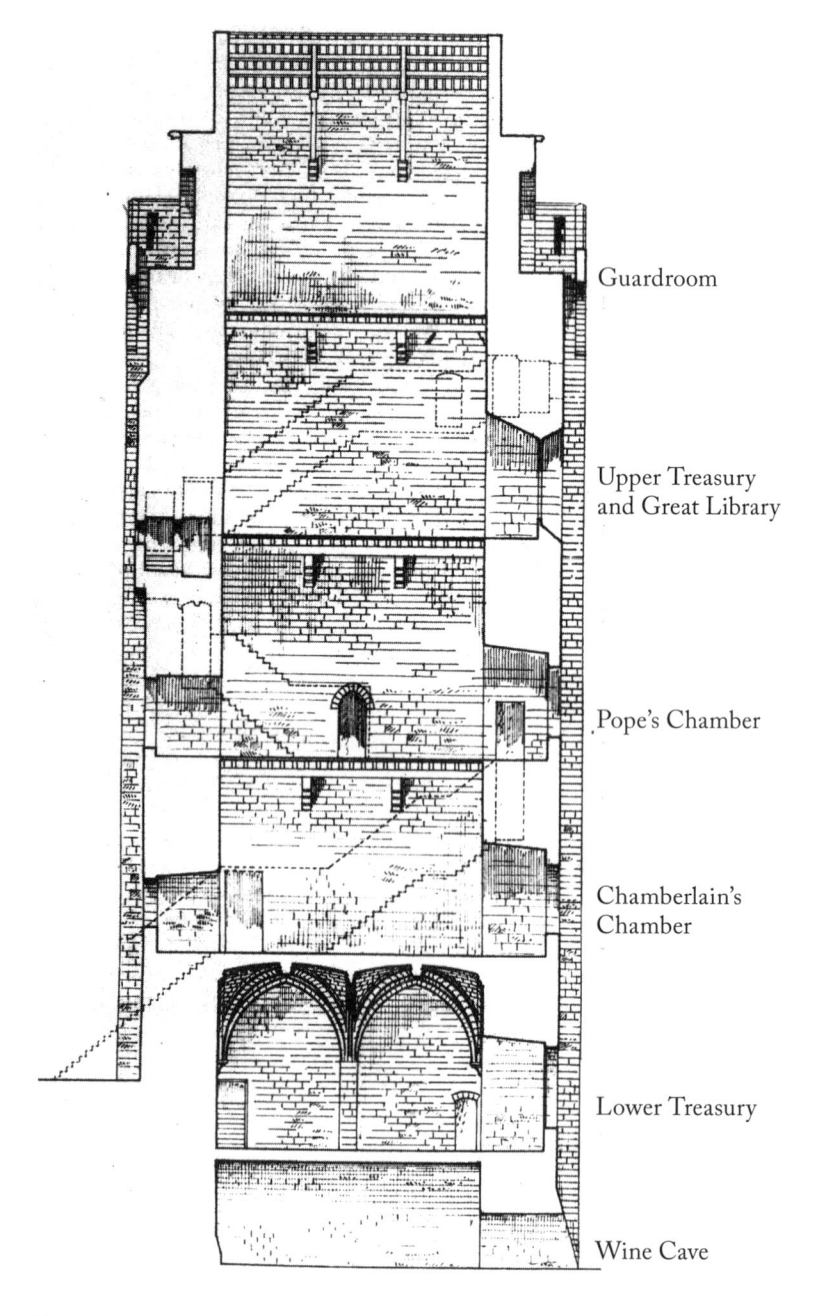

FIGURE 2.1
Pope's Tower in Section Viewed from the South.
Labande, *Palais des papes* (1925)

Such were the enormous papal powers granted to Pierre de Cros by *Apostolice Camere*. It is no exaggeration to say that the pope thereby delegated to him all his executive and judicial powers. The salutations of his letters (e.g., Calendar no. 7) often cite the source of his power by bidding the receiver "to obey our — nay, rather the apostolic — commands." The location of the chamberlain's bedchamber in the palace, connected to the pope's above by a single secret flight of stairs, further dramatized the plenitude of his authority.[10]

2. Treasury Chamber Court

The chamberlain's ordinary tribunal was named Treasury Chamber after the room where it sat. Gabriel Colombe argued convincingly that this was located in the Great Treasury, the ceilinged workroom, 190 meters square, beneath the Jesus Hall in the Eastern Wing of Private Apartments, and next to the Lower Treasury in the Pope's Tower.[11]

Because of the summary, largely oral procedure of the chamberlain's court, the causes heard there did not generate many written records. We do have some *procurationes*, that is, formal powers of attorney for particular causes before him.[12] The chamberlain, sitting in Treasury Chamber, did not have to arrive at a formal sentence embodied in a notarial instrument. Instead, a process was likely to end with the defendant's oral confession of debt, usually a negotiated settlement or *compositio*, and this would be confirmed with an *obligatio*, a plain bond which could be enforced by any court, and which we would find registered in the Vatican Archives series Obligationes et Solutiones. Often too there would be an executory letter, by which the chamberlain would settle any other business incidental to the cause. Copied into his own registers, many of those executory letters are to be found in this Calendar. Pierre de Cros made even more use of the powers of summary justice in Treasury Chamber than had his predecessor, for whom they

---

[10] Early in 1373 de Cros was living in a house of his own in Avignon, perhaps for greater comfort in the winter. His room in the Pope's Tower continued to be called *camera camerarii*, indicating his office space. Vingtain, *Avignon: Le Palais des Papes*, 106 and 238–39 states that from the time of Clement VI the chamberlain resided elsewhere, in the Great Dignitaries' Wing over the Champeaux gate, while the Chamberlain's Chamber in the Pope's Tower was used by squires, but I find no good evidence for the claim.

[11] The names and locations of the rooms were worked out by Gabriel Colombe, "La 'Grande Trésorerie' au Palais apostolique d'Avignon," in *Miscellanea Francesco Ehrle* (Vatican City, 1924), 2:504–23, illustrated with a plan (522). There is a good functional description of the Great Treasury in Vingtain, *Avignon: Le Palais des Papes*, 125–28, not including the courts of the chamberlain and auditor. The plan shown here is abridged from Labande, *Le palais des papes et les monuments d'Avignon au XIVe siècle*.

[12] An example is IM 2820, dated 26 January 1375, by which Johannes Baugerii de Vienes warranted a proctor to negotiate his canonry in the church of S. Sauveur (Aix).

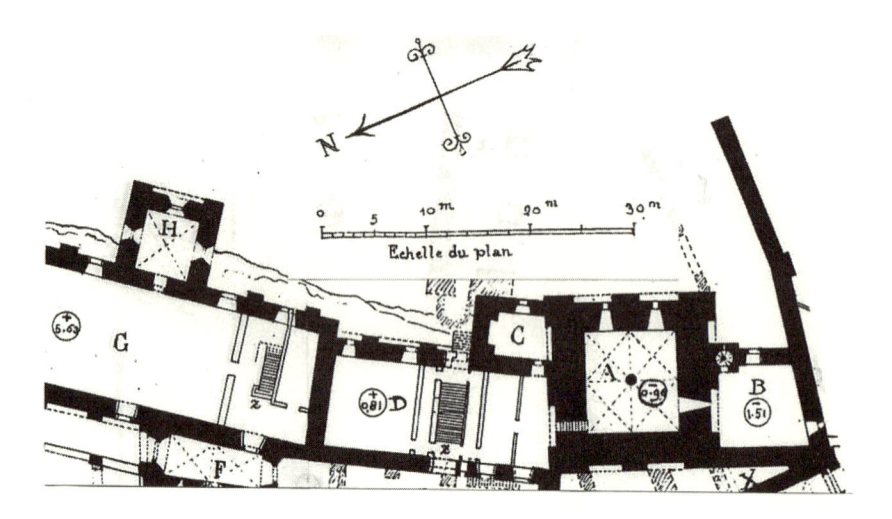

A: Pope's Tower, Lower Treasury; B: Wardrobe Tower; C: Study Tower, Secret Chamber; D: Great Treasury Chamber; F: Public passage to Treasury; G: Grand Tinel; H: Chapel of S. Martial

FIGURE 2.2
Plan of the Palace at Avignon: the Treasury Area.
After Labande, *Palais des Papes* (1925)

were designed.[13] The Topical Index to the Calendar shows procedural references to twenty-nine causes summoned or settled before the chamberlain in Treasury Chamber.

The ordinary *actor* or prosecutor of causes in the Treasury Chamber was the procurator fiscal. Even today this title from Roman civil law is that of a public prosecutor in Scotland. The chamberlain's sentences and executory letters often mentioned this officer (usually without giving his name) as the complainant who had begun a process in the Treasury Chamber. Two procurators fiscal appear under Pierre de Cros: Jacques Arnanesse, whose service began under Urban V,[14] and his lieutenant Tommaso da Ficucchio, once Sienese proctor in the Curia, who replaced him late in 1375.[15] Tommaso had his own lieutenant, Giovanni da

---

[13] Daniel Williman, "Summary Justice in the Avignonese Camera," in *Proceedings of the Sixth International Congress of Medieval Canon Law*, ed. Stephan Kuttner (Vatican City, 1985), 437–49.

[14] Guillemain, *La Cour*, 292, n. 82, citing EFR *Urbain V secrètes France*, no. 2684; Bernard Guillemain, "Les tribunaux de la cour pontificale d'Avignon," in *L'Eglise et le droit dans le Midi (XIIIe-XIVe s.)* (Toulouse, 1994), 339–60, esp. 353–54 for Jacques Arnanesse.

[15] Guillemain, *La Cour*, 145, n. 262; 570, n. 50.

Reggio, at work as a special prosecutor securing the confiscated property of the Florentines in Avignon in 1376 (Calendar no. 617).

The *advocatus Camere* Jacopo di Ceva acted as substitute for the procurator fiscal in 1376, prosecuting the cause against the Florentine Comune to the Interdict of 31 March 1376 and beyond (Calendar no. 548 and note). Some of the papal provinces required an officer with the same title, a military *avoué* in the old sense of a champion, for the local service of the Camera. We find Antonio Pochepen of Ravenna and Francesco de Capulis of Perugia received into service with this title early in the pontificate of Gregory XI.[16]

There were no exceptions to the universal competence of the chamberlain's tribunal. Even the auditors of the Rota, otherwise exempt from ecclesiastical censures, were subject to his, according to a chancery regulation of 10 June 1371.[17] The date is interesting, one day before the death of Arnaud Aubert, who had sternly corrected the auditors as a group back in 1364.[18]

B. Personnel and Administration of the Camera

1. Treasurer

Gaucelme de Déaux, bishop of Maguelonne, became apostolic treasurer under Urban V in 1362. Remaining behind when the Curia of Urban V went to Italy, he supervised the finances, with special attention to Urban's new college at Montpellier. His commission was not renewed after Urban's death, but he stayed in touch with the administration, and when he died in 1373 Pierre de Cros had a special responsibility for the collection of his spoils.[19]

Pierre de Vernols, abbot of Aniane, had served Urban V and the chamberlain Arnaud Aubert as treasurer. His office too lapsed with Urban's death, and he took it up again "at the customary wages" immediately after the election of Gregory XI, swearing the usual oath to the chamberlain (still Arnaud Aubert) on 3 January 1371.[20] Bishop of Maguelonne after the death of Gaucelme de Déaux in 1373, Pierre de Vernols continued in the office of treasurer through the pontificate of Gregory XI. He stayed behind to direct financial affairs in Avignon

---

[16] RA 173, 61v.

[17] Emil von Ottenthal, *Regulae cancellariae apostolicae: Die päpstlichen Kanzleiregeln von Johannes XXII. bis Nicolaus V.* (Innsbruck, 1888; repr. Aalen, 1968), 33: Gregory XI, rule no. 52.

[18] Aubert Calendar no. 238, 161–62.

[19] Hoberg, *Inventare*, 486; EFR *Grégoire XI secrètes France*, no. 1355.

[20] RA 173, 51r, where he is inaccurately designated "tunc abbas monasterii de Salmo," i.e., of Psalmody. The entry must have been written in 1373 or later, but the notaries were frequently uncertain of Vernols' abbey, giving "de Aghanna" and "de Anhano" in 1371: Hoberg, *Inventare*, 486, 496.

when the chamberlain accompanied the pope to Italy in 1376.[21] Pierre de Cros himself, after declaring the Apostolic See vacant, renewed Vernols' commission as treasurer in the summer of 1378.[22] He died in office in 1389.

All the personnel of the Camera Apostolica answered to the chamberlain, especially the treasurer, whose punctilious reports of *introitus et exitus* were designed to sustain the chamberlain's scrutiny in monthly and annual audits.[23] Pierre de Vernols had to report at the end of each year of service (as of 4 January) what moneys the Treasury had taken in and paid out, and the balance of cash on hand. Of course the economic activities of the College of Cardinals, and many of those of the Camera Apostolica, neither paid into the Treasury at Avignon nor drew out of it, and so many large transactions in money and other values do not appear in the treasurer's balance. Nevertheless, it is in the treasurer's accounts that we come closest to an annual budget of the central government of the Church.

On 6 March 1372 Pierre de Cros and the clerks of the Camera formally related their approval of the accounts kept by Pierre de Vernols for the first year of Gregory XI, ending 4 January 1372. The pope then accepted the account and acquitted Vernols of all debt to the Camera. The balance in the Treasury was 3787 Cameral florins and 14,861 francs; expense from the Treasury had somewhat exceeded income, both in the neighborhood of 300,000 florins.[24] In the next four years the annual budgets roughly balanced, rising to about 600,000 florins (January 1374) and then falling off again.[25] These are rough estimates. The treasurer's accounts gave both income and expense in more than a dozen gold coinages, some more and some less valuable than the standard Cameral florin, though the silver money was almost all in deniers of Avignon.

The complexity of the currency required a specialist, for example Raimond de Chazeilles, in the "officium percipiendi, administrandi et solvendi pecunias," a cashier in short.[26] The duties of the receiver Guillaume Gloire, canon of Lodève, a trusty familiar and proctor of Gaucelme de Déaux, must have been similar; in 1364 he had picked out of the spoils of the bishop of Majorca a fine

---

[21] Johann Peter Kirsch, *Die Rückkehr der Päpste Urban V. und Gregor XI. von Avignon nach Rom* (Paderborn, 1898), xxv.

[22] Coll. 393, 70v and 73r, repeated 92v-93r.

[23] These ledgers or *Hauptbücher* are the focus of an accurate and useful study by Stefan Weiss, *Rechnungswesen und Buchhaltung des Avignoneser Papsttums (1316–1378): Eine Quellenkunde* (Hannover, 2003); see esp. 167–75 and 240–46 for the time of Pierre de Vernols.

[24] EFR *Grégoire XI secrètes France*, no. 668; VQ 6:353–55.

[25] Account of early 1373, VQ 6:376–78; early 1374, VQ 6:435–37; early 1375, VQ 6:495; early 1376, VQ 6:567.

[26] Calendar no. 617; Guillemain, *La Cour*, 289, n. 61.

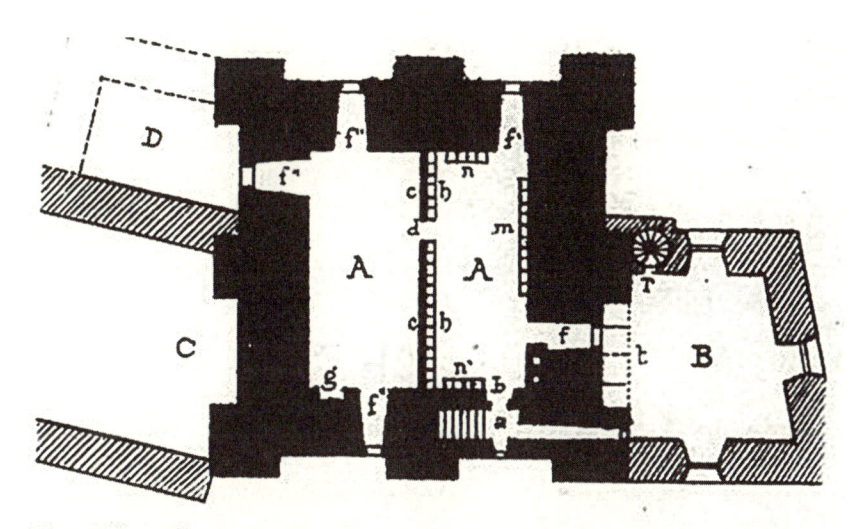

Quatrième étage de la Tour des Anges, d'après le Dr Colombe.
Trésorerie haute (à gauche) et Bibliothèque (à droite).— B. Tour de la Garde-robe. — C. Aile des appartements privés. — D. Tour de l'Etude (plus basse). — *a.* Palier de l'escalier venant de la chambre du Pape. — *b.* Porte d'entrée. — *c.* Cloison séparant la Trésorerie de la Bibliothèque. — *d.* Passage entre les deux appartements. — *f.* Fenêtres primitives. — *g.* Cheminée. — *h. m. n.* Rayons de la Bibliothèque.

FIGURE 2.3
Upper Treasury and Great Library
Labande, *Palais des Papes* (1925)

pair of silk-and-silver scales, for the use of the Camera, and he was usually present at weighings in the Treasury with Pierre de Vernols.[27]

The treasurer was also responsible for such precious objects as gold and silver vessels, both consecrated and secular, reliquaries, rings and other jewelry. These were checked into and out of the Treasury and occasionally surveyed in a thorough inventory.[28] Books too were kept by the Treasury until they were sold, given away, or (by the time of Gregory XI) sent up to the research library above the pope's bedchamber. A wooden partition divided that tower room into northern and southern halves, the Great Library with its four walls of bookstacks to the south and the Upper Treasury to the north, where precious objects were kept in armaria.[29]

---

[27] Aubert Calendar 152, no. 209; Calendar nos. 20, 39, 175; Hoberg, *Inventare*, 523–27.

[28] For our period, Hoberg's *Inventare* has three long documents: inventories in the first years of Gregory XI (465–517), inventory of the stables, May 1371 (518–22), and records of removals from the Treasury between 1371 and 1376 (523–41).

[29] From Labande, *Le palais des papes et les monuments d'Avignon au XIVe siècle*, 1:100.

The rest of the treasure was kept in the Lower Treasury just below the chamberlain's lodging in the Pope's Tower, partly in rectangular stone coffers under the limestone slabs of the floor, along the north and south walls, in the spaces secretly left unfilled in the barrel-vaulting of the wine cave below. Among the few fragments found there when the chests were opened in 1985 was a part of a bishop's seal, likely that of the treasurer Pierre de Vernols as bishop of Maguelonne 1373–1389, and likely broken off a chest rather than from a letter. The stone coffers continued in use under Clement VII, one of whose lead bulls was also found there.[30]

2. Auditor of the Camera

The auditor or judge was an officer of the pre-Avignonese Camera. His court, the *Auditio Camere*, had been responsible for the great mass of legal business in the Camera before Innocent VI, but in the present records we see more of the chamberlain himself as judge than of the auditor. Pierre Villain de Paris, dean of Gap and a papal chaplain, became auditor general of the Camera on 23 December 1369, and he still held the office in 1378.[31] During Villain's service as nuncio in Castile and Portugal, there seems to have been a vice-auditor of the Camera (Calendar no. 169). Villain died in 1389, bishop of Lombez.[32] The auditor had a seal and a seal-bearer, and he kept a prison which the chamberlain used when necessary (Calendar no. 515). A Chancery regulation of 16 November 1374 strengthened the auditor's power of arrest by forbidding a debtor to confess by proxy if he was present in the Curia.[33]

---

[30] Sylvain Gagnière, "Le Trésor bas dans la Tour du Pape: fouilles et restauration," *Annuaire de la Société des Amis du Palais des Papes* 71–72 (1984–1985): 45–65. See also Vingtain, *Avignon: Le Palais des Papes*, 101–6 for the Lower Treasury, with plates XIV-XVII.

[31] RA 198, 460v; Dykmans, "La fin du séjour," 19, n. 5.

[32] Williman, *Right of Spoil*, 216, no. 979, with the mis-designation "auditor sacri palatii."

[33] Ottenthal, *Regulae*, 38–39: Gregory XI, rule no. 67. See Guillemain, "Les tribunaux," 352–54 for the auditor of the Camera and a description of his seal, though Pierre Villain is not mentioned there.

3. Clerks and Councillors of the Camera

Eleven clerks of the Camera served under Gregory XI.[34] Four of these, already in service under Urban V, preserved administrative continuity; we see them at work in the Treasury at the beginning of the pontificate.[35] Eblo de Miers, a veteran from the time of Clement VI who had been with the Camera in Italy through 1368 and 1369, appears to be superannuated but still standing as a witness early in 1371; then he retired to the bishopric of Vaison.[36] Pierre Dalbiartz had gone to Italy with the Camera of Arnaud Aubert in 1367.[37] He was a valuable specialist in the business of annates in Germany, work which was taken over by his senior colleague Maurice de la Barde (who had stayed at Avignon 1367–1370). Maurice was first mentioned in 1362, last on 21 May 1376. Guillaume Atbert became a clerk 12 January 1363, served as treasurer of the gabelles of Avignon from 1366, and was last mentioned in Cameral service 6 March 1372; he died 12 March 1373.[38]

Two other clerks began their service early in the pontificate of Gregory XI. Elie de Vodron, formerly clerk of the College of Cardinals, swore his oath to Arnaud Aubert on 7 February 1371, and the next day was inducted as a chaplain of honor and apostolic notary; he supervised the inventory of the stables and the payment of Urban V's funeral expenses.[39] He was the first clerk of the Camera with a detached assignment, as special nuncio to collect a tenth from Germany against the Visconti from 5 April 1372 into early 1374. Back in Avignon early in 1375, he witnessed the treasurer's annual accounting.[40] Vodron went to Perugia and Rome in September 1375 to help prepare for the return of the Curia to Italy, using the title vice-treasurer or *gerens officii thesaurarii sedis apostolice*.[41] Then he was the first clerk to be promoted bishop (of Catania in Sicily, 14 May 1376) while remaining clerk and vice-treasurer, and in the latter capacity he accompanied the chamberlain on the Curia's voyage to Italy. After the two elections of 1378 he is found in the court of Clement VII. Pierre Girard was a trusted servant of Gregory XI

---

[34] François Baix, "Notes sur les clercs de la Chambre apostolique (13e-14e siècles)," *Bulletin de l'Institut historique belge de Rome* 27 (1952): 42–47 has the best list, though it is not quite complete.

[35] Hoberg, *Inventare*, 465 for Maurice de la Barde and Pierre Dalbiartz in the Lower Treasury, 8 January 1371; 486 for Guillaume Atbert and Eblo de Miers in the Upper Treasury on the 27th; 496 for Pierre and Eblo on 5 February.

[36] Aubert Calendar, 29; Williman, *Right of Spoil*, 96, no. 260.

[37] In VQ 6 Pierre Dalbiartz is mentioned from 1365 to 1373.

[38] These notes come from the fichier of Curial functionaries compiled by Anne-Marie Hayez. For Guillaume Atbert see *Fasti ecclesiae Gallicanae* 8, Diocèse de Mende, 184, no. 10.

[39] RA 173, 51r; Hoberg, *Inventare*, 518.

[40] VQ 6:495.

[41] Paul Maria Baumgarten, *Aus Kanzlei und Kammer* (Freiburg im Breisgau, 1907), 59 n.; Theiner 2, no. 591; Segrè, ed., "I dispacci," 79 and 83.

and the first new clerk who swore his oath to Pierre de Cros, on 21 August 1371. When the Curia departed for Italy it was Pierre Girard who arranged lodging for it at Marseille; then he returned to Avignon briefly to serve the treasurer Pierre de Vernols.[42] Gregory XI sent Girard from Rome on a special mission to his brother Guillaume de Beaufort, viscount of Turenne, in December 1377. Girard joined the court of Clement VII, represented the Camera in France on a long mission, then became bishop of Lodève and finally cardinal in 1390.[43]

Before his brief service as clerk, Guillaume de Prohins had been a Cameral notary. Clerk at least from 23 March 1373, he left the office to become bishop of Mirepoix 3 July 1377, and died shortly afterwards. His brother Gui de Prohins, a knight in the service of Urban V and Gregory XI, was senator, the pope's military governor of Rome, when Gregory died and the elections were held which began the Schism.

Bertrand Raffin had been a familiar of the treasurer Gaucelme de Déaux, and had supervised the building works of Urban V at Montpellier. Then collector of Narbonne, he traveled to Germany on Cameral business in September 1372, and he appears as clerk by 2 March 1375. Raffin was probably the clerk who was sent to Germany in December 1375 to negotiate for mercenary troops against the rebellions in the States of the Church, according to Cristoforo Tolomei.[44] With the title of vicar general in Rome, Viterbo, and Montefiascone, he left Avignon on 2 April 1376 to act as *taxator domorum* and to secure the cardinals' customary *librate* or palaces in Rome.[45] By that time, Viterbo and Montefiascone were out of the question because of their rebellion. Raffin represented the Camera in negotiations with Robert d'Hauteville, captain of mercenaries in the service of Queen Joan of Naples, in November 1376.[46] He rejoined the Camera of Pierre de Cros when it came to Italy, and after the twin elections of 1378 he joined the court of Clement VII; he became bishop of Rodez in January 1379.

Three clerks of the Camera, appointed at Avignon in 1376 and 1377, had no dealings with the chamberlain that I have seen in his letters; they seem to have worked only with the treasurer. Seguin d'Authon was a clerk by 11 October 1374, and he died Latin titular patriarch of Antioch in 1380.[47] Pierre Borrier was added to the clerks on 1 September 1377, and his service under Clement VII seems

---

[42] Kirsch, *Rückkehr*, xxv.

[43] Favier, *Finances*, 60; EFR *Grégoire XI secrètes France*, no. 2100.

[44] Segrè, ed., "I dispacci," 83.

[45] His list of cardinals and their *librate* in 1378, misattributed to Elie de Vodron, is edited in Baumgarten, *Aus Kanzlei und Kammer*, 59–61.

[46] Kirsch, *Rückkehr*, xxv; RA 200, 644r-645r is the contract, dated 30 November 1376 and witnessed by Bertrand du Mazel, for 200 lances of 3 horses each with 100 mounted Hungarian archers, an escort for the reception of the pope.

[47] Favier, *Finances*, 60.

to have been as legate in Aragon.[48] Gasbert de Longanh is mentioned 1 December 1377, and then under Clement VII; he died before 23 February 1385.[49]

The clerks worked singly to supervise particular fiscal transactions and accounts, and to draft the letters incidental to those cases for the chamberlain's seal. Their signatures appear on the fold of the original letters, but their names are seldom noted in the registers. The clerks all together constituted a Cameral Council, and in various groupings formed committees of account headed by the chamberlain or the auditor of the Camera, before whom the collectors and the treasurer reported their activities and records, and they witnessed the instruments of recognition and quittance which followed those examinations. The lowest room of the Study Tower, connected to the Great Treasury and Lower Treasury, was their Secret Chamber, a room where the current registers of the Camera were kept and adjacent to the space in the Lower Treasury where the Council met.[50] A supernumerary councillor, usually a lawyer, appears occasionally in this group at Avignon: Sicard de Bruguerol, licentiate of decrees, is found in this role but without the title in 1375 and 1377; and we see Jean Cabrespi, doctor of decrees, with the descriptive title "Apostolice Camere consiliarius, auditor et examinator computorum," anticipating the current English meaning of "auditor," an expert judge of accounts. Jean Cabrespi went ahead of the Curia to Rome, departing Avignon on 9 July 1376 with the furnishings of the pope's chapel.[51]

4. Notaries

It appears that the formal writing of the Camera from 1371 to 1378 was the work of two notaries public, both veterans of the Camera of Arnaud Aubert.[52] They engrossed and sealed the chamberlain's letters and notarial instruments, writing their own names on their work, and they registered the letters as well. Jacques de

---

[48] EFR *Grégoire XI secrètes France*, no. 2021; cf. Lily Greiner, "Un représentant de la Chambre apostolique de Clément VII en Aragon au début du Grand Schisme (1378–1380)," *Mélanges* 65 (1953): 197–214.

[49] Favier, *Finances*, 60.

[50] Vingtain, *Avignon: Le Palais des Papes*, 132–33. Fausto Piola Caselli, "L'evoluzione della contabilità camerale nel periodo avignonese," in *Aux origines de l'état moderne*, 411–37, here 433, n. 63 points out that the Study Tower room itself was too small for a Council attended by six clerks.

[51] Segrè, ed., "I dispacci," 92; Jean Cabrespi's accounts as collector of England, 1363–1371, are edited by William E. Lunt, *Accounts Rendered by Papal Collectors in England* (Philadelphia, 1968), 172–362.

[52] A Symonetus Fay appears once, witnessing an extraction from the Treasury in June 1373 (Hoberg, *Inventare*, 537) and qualified as notary and secretary of the chamberlain. He belonged to the private rather than the official staff of Pierre de Cros.

Solèges had joined the staff in 1361 as a substitute, to engross instruments from the notes of four recently deceased notaries (it was a plague year). He was with the Curia of Urban V in Italy; in fact, he drafted the 1367 League of Viterbo. He succeeded Jean Palaysin in the special task of drafting and registering instruments of obligation. With the Camera in Italy once more, he witnessed the submission of Bologna in 1377 (Calendar nos. 258 and 625).

Jean Rousset had been subcollector and then briefly collector in Lyon-Vienne, and had been charged with some provisions of victuals to the Curia. He appears first as a notary of the Camera in 1368 at Montefiascone, drafting instruments of contract and registering them in his own portfolio, the traditional practice of a notary public but a novelty in the Camera. Rousset's special register until April 1372 was the volume now designated Collectoriae 357; after 1373 and into the schism period, he used RA 220, perhaps not to the exclusion of other registrars. Beyond his notarial work, Rousset received special commissions, to gather the spoils of the late treasurer Gaucelme de Déaux and again to supervise the shipment of provisions from Burgundy (Calendar nos. 347 and 434). A colleague, Johannes de Siccacuria, joined him as signing notary in the chamberlain's visas of the imperial bulls against the Visconti (Calendar nos. 183 and 185). Rousset joined his colleague Solèges in registering *obligationes*, and both went to Italy with Pierre de Cros.

5. Money, Bankers, Exchange, Loans

The chamberlain appointed the provost of the mint of Avignon and received his oath (Calendar no. 5), but Pierre de Cros does not seem to have given any directions for the operation of the mint. The exchange values recognized by Cardinal Philippe Cabassole as rector of the Comtat Venaissin in 1369 remained close to constant because the Camera, the mint, and the Treasury all supported them.[53]

The silver coins of Gregory XI from Avignon imitated the old carlins of Provence. They picture the pope on a lion-head throne; Roger roses appear on his cope and in the inscription. These carlins were called *grossi* in the accounts, but by 1369 the name seems to mean only that they were nearly pure silver, by contrast with the fractional coinage struck on billon in the same mint for local use.[54]

---

[53] RA 198, 496, ed. Gino Arias, "La chiesa e la storia economica del Medio Evo," *Archivio della Reale Società di Storia Patria* 29 (1906): 145–81, here 169–70.

[54] Allen G. Berman, *Papal Coins* (South Salem, NY, 1991), 57 and plate 6, no. 213 for the carlin; nos. 214–216 for billon coins. This repertory has inaccurate historical information and its coin exhibits and plates are not entirely clear, but it is more complete than its predecessors, especially for gold and billon coins. The carlin is shown in copperplate by Faustin Poey d'Avant, *Monnaies féodales de France*, 4 vols. (Paris, 1858–1862), 2: planche XCIV no. 4, but the reverse of the coin was printed mirror-backward, and so copied by Berman. The carlin shown here is from Camillo Serafini, *Le monete e le bolle*

Administration of the Camera Apostolica 1371–1378

- ✱ - GREGORV � - ⁏ PP ⁏ VΠDEO' ✱
intorno da d. in alto a sin.
Il Pont. sedente di faccia su trono adorno di due protomi di leoni in senso contrario con tiara e piviale con fibbia a rosetta, benedicente, tiene nella sin. lunga asta su cui crocetta nel giro; entro doppio cord. circ. int. ed est.

✱ ⋈ ⁏ SANCTVS ⋈ ⁏ PETRVS ⁏ ⋈ intorno incominc. in alto.
Grandi chiavi decuss. e legate; entro doppio cord. circ. int. ed est.

FIGURE 2.4
Carlin or Gros of Gregory XI.
From Serafini, *Le monete* (1910).

In diameter 26 mm. and about 2.84 grams in weight, the *denarius grossus* of Avignon was the only silver coin which the Treasury would accept. Assignments to the Camera, like payments into the English Exchequer, had to be "blanched," converted into the purer silver of the sovereign's mint. Accounts of the Camera were recorded in florins, *solidi*, and *denarii*. The *denarii* were these silver *gros*; a *solidus* or *sou* was a count of twelve *gros*, not a coin; and the Cameral gold florin was valued at a whole number of *solidi* of Avignon, 26 *solidi* (or 312 *gros*) in 1369.

Since 1322 the Avignon mint had also struck a fine gold coinage, the florins of the Camera. These were practically identical to the florins of Florence in measure, design, and value. Nominally fine, that is, as near 24-karat as they could be made by smelting, 63 Cameral florins were struck from a mark of metal (222.5 grams), so that their average weight was 3.53 grams, their diameter 21 mm. After 1374, when Florence became an enemy, the image of John the Baptist and the stylized lily, emblems of Florence, disappeared from the papal florins. On the obverse of the only florin of Gregory XI known to survive we see the pope on a throne decorated with lions' heads, with two Roger roses in the inscription and six more surrounding the floral cross on the reverse, with the motto "Christus vincit, regit, imperat."[55]

Less valuable florins called *floreni currentes*, worth 21 to 24 *solidi* of Avignon, also appear in the records, and some such florins were actually minted at Avignon.

---

plombee pontificie del Medagliere Vaticano (Milan, 1910), 1, Tavola XII, no. 19; the description from p. 79.

[55] Serafini, *Le monete*, 1, Tavola XII, no. 18, described p. 79.

- • GREGORIV ⁚ PP ◦ - • VNDECIMƷ
intorno da d. in alto a sin.
Il Pont. sedente di faccia e benedicente con tiara, abiti pontificali ed asta crucigera nella sin.; entro cordone int. a doppia centina, e cord. circ. est.

✱ ⁚+⁚ RECT ⁚+⁚VICIT ⁚+⁚ II I·I PTT ⁚
intorno incominc. in alto.
Grande croce gigliata con quattro rosette alle estremità, negli spazi a d. in alto ed a sin. in basso due paia di chiavette decussate e legate in fuori, nei restanti due rosette; entro lin. circ. int. e cord. circ. est.

FIGURE 2.5
Cameral Florin of Gregory XI.
From Serafini, Le monete (1910)

The coined image of the pope enthroned strikingly echoes a life-size 14th-century limestone figure of St. Peter in the Museum of Fine Arts, Boston.[56]

A Camera which had to receive and pay large sums at great distances had alternative means of doing so which can be crisply expressed: assignment or transfer? And if transfer, by letter of exchange or by transport of cash?[57]

Of course, all the uncoined gold and silver and other precious objects had to be transported to the Treasury; and most of the coin came the same way, on the backs of horses and mules. This was the wealth of Languedoc and France, the lifeblood of the Avignon Curia. Robbery was a hazard, but less so in the 1370s than it later became, and less in Languedoc and Provence than, for example, in Sardinia and the kingdom of Naples (Calendar nos. 207, 541, 609).

Letters of *cambium* or exchange were the late medieval response to the uncertainty of the roads, and the Camera made much use of them, especially for transfers to the Treasury from England, the Low Countries, and Iberia, and for payments out of the Treasury to creditors in Italy, usually for war.

The letter of exchange served as an international money order. A collector would pay his money, in any mix of currencies, for example to a merchant at Bruges who was the factor or agent of an international merchant company. The collector would receive back a letter promising that another factor of the same company would pay a certain fixed sum in gold, on or after a certain day, at Avignon. The collector would carry or send his letter to Avignon, while the Bruges factor sent a copy of the contract to the Avignon factor, to notify him of the coming need to have the gold ready and as a counterfoil by which to verify the collector's

---

[56] Color photographs can be found on the compact disk enclosed in this book.
[57] Favier, *Finances*, chaps. 8 and 9.

letter when this should be presented. The collector or a clerk of the Camera would present the letter, take the gold, and return a receipt for it. The merchant company's fee and profit would be in the difference between the value of the moneys paid over by the collector at Bruges and the value of the gold counted out at Avignon. The Alberti Antichi of Florence had nearly a monopoly of the Camera's international transfer business at the end of Urban V's pontificate, but Pierre de Cros did not foster this cooperation; instead he permitted collectors to arrange their own letters of exchange with any available merchant. Andrea Tici da Pistoia, who operated a modest number of agencies from his bank at Avignon, did as much Cameral business as he could (Calendar nos. 575 and 638). In 1376 the war with Florence definitely ended the Curia's link with the Alberti, and late that year Gregory XI gave a warrant to Francesco and Nicolo dei Guinigi, merchant bankers of Lucca, to receive funds from papal collectors either at Venice or at Bruges. Pierre de Cros favored in the same way the factors of Andrea Tici, at least those who took in the receipts of England at Bruges.[58]

Pierre de Cros did move the Camera's wealth by pack-mule and by letter of exchange, but he came to favor assignment, that is, a letter granting the ownership of Cameral moneys to a creditor of the Camera. Future as well as current fiscal receipts could be assigned; the right (and the trouble) of collecting what was due to the Camera could itself be transferred. Collectors' accounts, under the heading *assignationes*, reveal many such transfers of property for which no other evidence survives, though they had to be ordered or approved by the Camera. Especially in 1374 and after, confronted by obligations which the Treasury was unable to pay, de Cros bypassed the Treasury and assigned present and future assets of the Camera, distant or near. The Calendar shows how often he resorted to this expedient of deficit finance, and what unseemly situations could follow from it. For example, large sums of church taxes were assigned to relatives of the pope, and then ecclesiastical incomes had to be surrendered by various collectories to laymen (Calendar nos. 367, 393, 570, 571, 602, 630, 639, 644). Even more scandalously, in a way, taxes taken from the clergy of Tuscany were granted in a blank check to pay for the shipment of eels from the "apostolic lake" of Bolsena (Calendar no. 436).

The exchange of currencies at Avignon and the weighing, estimation, and exchange of worked gold and silver were largely entrusted to *campsores* or changers, sometimes characterized as merchants following the Roman Curia. Three Italians were most prominent in this work: Andrea Tici of Pistoia, whom we saw above as a banker of the Curia, and the Florentines Giovanni Baroncelli and Cristoforo Gieri, the latter a papal sergeant at arms as well. The heavy lifting and the armed security required in the Treasury meant that the clerical staff of

---

[58] EFR *Grégoire XI secrètes autres*, no. 3958; see esp. Calendar nos. 625, 626 and footnotes.

the Curia had to welcome in some sergeants and ushers, all of whom had sworn their honest loyalty to the chamberlain.

The changers were constantly involved when precious objects from the Treasury were pawned, sometimes as assayers, weighers, and witnesses, sometimes even as brokers, safekeepers, or lenders. The chamberlain was compelled to borrow, using the treasure as security, many times. Most often the loan came from a living cardinal or from the executors (very often including Pierre de Cros himself) of the estate of a deceased cardinal; in this way some of the profits which cardinals had derived from the beneficial system could be used in the pope's interest, without any imputation of confiscation or right of spoil over the College. Some of these loan debts were probably forgiven as time went on and the state of the Camera remained poor. It will be instructive to review the most important loans secured by pawns from the Treasury.[59] But we should first note that the large loans of Louis duke of Anjou in 1376 and 1377, considered in the next chapter, were another matter entirely: they did not involve the chamberlain directly, and they were secured only by the pope's word, not by his treasure.

Pierre de Cros himself, before his appointment as chamberlain, had advanced 9000 florins from the estate of Cardinal Nicolas de Besse (who died at Rome in 1369) to help pay the expenses of the Curia's return to Avignon. He partially secured that debt in 1372 with a selection of crafted gold, mostly pectoral brooches, weighing 37 marks (if coined, the metal would have yielded only 2331 florins). The pawned goldware remained in the palace, in a chest secured with the chamberlain's great seal and placed in a room under the Pope's Study in the Study Tower, that is, the Secret Chamber next to the Lower Treasury.[60] The pawn was presumably returned to the Treasury on 8 August 1373 when the loan was repaid, apparently with 10% interest, an extra 953 *chaises d'or*.[61]

On 18 August 1372, in anticipation of the revenues of midsummer, Gregory XI granted Pierre de Cros a warrant to borrow 50,000 florins, using goods of the treasure as security. The permission was repeated in a second warrant the next year, on 24 September 1373.[62] Acting on his first special warrant, in October 1372, de Cros borrowed for the Treasury a total of 48,000 florins and 5000 francs from the estate (of which he was administrator) of Hugues Roger, the cardinal-chamberlain who had died in 1363 in possession of vast sums from undistributed services. The goldware set aside as a pawn, in the same way as before, weighed 780 marks, quite close to the weight of the florins and francs borrowed. De Cros actually paid into the Treasury 35,000 florins and the 5000 francs im-

---

[59] Hermann Hoberg edited the indispensable document, Collectoriae 468, 133r-147v, in *Inventare*, 523–41.

[60] 25 September 1372: Hoberg, *Inventare*, 531–32.

[61] VQ 6:446.

[62] *Cum pro certis arduis* and *Cum pro necessitate Camere*, cited and edited respectively in EFR *Grégoire XI secrètes France*, nos. 2634 and 1393.

mediately, and 10,000 florins the next April. I have not seen that he ever accounted for the 3000 extra florins for which he had obligated the Camera.[63]

Claiming to have a mandate of the pope which was apparently not written, de Cros continued to borrow on pawn through the first half of 1373. Two crosses and a reliquary (34 marks of gold) and 1608 marks of silver goods went to Cardinal Guillaume d'Aigrefeuille the younger against loans of 8000 florins. Returned to the Treasury in May 1376, the three gold items were pawned again immediately to Cardinal Pierre de la Jugie for 2000 florins.[64] In March 1373, again mentioning but not showing a mandate of the pope, de Cros took 27 gold items from the Upper Treasury to be pawned for the wars in Lombardy, a total of 184 marks (about 41 kilograms): enough to secure 11,600 florins. The lenders or brokers were the changers Tici, Gieri, and Baroncelli, and they moved the pawned goldware out of the palace to their own houses, later consolidating the deposit in Gieri's house.[65] On 1 June de Cros took out the grand jeweled cross which King John of France had given to Clement VI, 76 marks' weight of gold, jewels, and enamels, and pawned it to Cardinal Raimond de Canilhac for 13,500 francs.[66]

On 27 September 1373, showing his second license to borrow 50,000 florins, de Cros permitted two merchants of Lucca to carry away 603 marks of goldware in two chests and a pannier. Many of the items had earlier been in the Hugues Roger pawn, perhaps redeemed subsequently, perhaps forgiven. The merchants were acting as agents of Jacopo Provana, knight of Turin, an officer of Count Amadeo VI of Savoy. The amount of the merchants' loan was not expressed but, to judge by the value of the pawn, it could have been in the neighborhood of 38,000 florins.[67]

After six months without pawning, we find 102 marks' weight of gold cups held by a merchant, a fair security for a loan of 6000 fl. by the executors of Cardinal Gui de Boulogne. In August 1375 the late cardinal's debts to the Camera for unpaid annates were charged, at 4000 francs, against the Camera's debt for the loan, and the executors accepted 800 francs as full payment of the rest. The pledge, now redeemed, was transferred to the agent of Amadeo of Savoy to secure 5000 florins owed to him for grain which he had provided to the besieged city of Vercelli.[68] The executors of Cardinal Etienne de Poissy who, like Gui de

---

[63] 12 October 1372: Hoberg, *Inventare*, 527–30, 535; *Analecta Vaticano-Belgica* 10:678.

[64] 4 January 1373: Hoberg, *Inventare*, 532–5.

[65] 12 March 1373: Hoberg, *Inventare*, 535–36; edited also by Léon Mirot, "Les rapports financiers de Grégoire XI et du duc d'Anjou," *Mélanges* 17 (1897): 113–44, here 126–27, although this transaction did not concern the duke.

[66] 1 June 1373: Hoberg, *Inventare*, 153, 536–37.

[67] 27 September 1373: Hoberg, *Inventare*, 530–31.

[68] 2 March 1374: Hoberg, *Inventare*, 537–39.

Boulogne, had died late in 1373, took 62 marks of goldware for their loan of 2974 florins and 916 francs.[69]

To recapitulate: following the first papal license to borrow 50,000 florins (August 1372) Pierre de Cros lent to the Treasury about 98,000 florins; following the second (September 1373) he borrowed for the Treasury about 53,000 florins. The *introitus et exitus* records of the Treasury have large gaps in the crucial years, but we know that these sums were at the disposal of the chamberlain and that the war in Lombardy against the brothers Visconti was the reason for the licenses to borrow. De Cros sent a last payment of 2045 fl. from the pope's house at Orgon to the war treasurer at Vercelli on 15 July 1374, just as he undertook his mission to negotiate a truce in that costly war.[70]

The last recorded extraction of treasure was for an assignment on the eve of the pope's voyage: Cardinal Robert of Geneva took three chests containing about 320 marks of goldware with which to pay a third monthly stipend of the men at arms being sent to Lombardy. No cash sum was stated, but the gold would have been good for over 20,000 florins.[71]

How improvidently Gregory XI was spending the Church's treasure is clearly demonstrated by his will, a nuncupative or oral testament which he declared on 5 May 1374 at Villeneuve, where he had taken refuge from the incipient plague in Avignon.[72] The pope breezily interpreted the distinction between personal and ecclesiastical wealth in his own favor and treated quantities of cash in careless generalities. Most of the text of the will is devoted to the statutes of a new Gregorian College of thirty Benedictine monks to be created within the community of Chaise-Dieu, with their own dormitory and prior's house, their own sacristan and chapel, under the floor of which his ashes would be entombed. There is no guess in the testament as to the cost of this magnificent living memorial and other foundations. They were to be paid for by liquidating all the pope's ecclesiastical real property and collecting 45,000 florins of debts due, two-thirds owed by the archbishop of Mainz for the fruits of the last vacancy and the rest as a promised subsidy by the Cistercians of Germany. Failing collection of those debts, subsidies from the clergy of England, Castile, and Portugal and debts due from Sicily, hopefully estimated at 200,000 florins, should be used. The pope recognized, though he did not quantify, the debts owed to the executors of deceased cardinals' testaments. He guaranteed repayment of the sums borrowed in the last two years, out of Cameral revenues because the funds were used to defend the lands of the Roman Church in Italy. If repayment was impossible, he permitted those creditors to keep or sell the pawned treasure. He insisted that any wealth

---

[69] 4 March 1374: Hoberg, *Inventare*, 539.

[70] VQ 6:587.

[71] 4 August 1376: Hoberg, *Inventare*, 540; also edited, less completely, by Mirot, "Les rapports," 127–28.

[72] Luc d'Achery, ed., *Spicilegium* (Paris, 1723), 3:738–42.

which he might have or get in the future from the property of his parents did not belong to the Church, but should go to his brothers and their heirs. He made the Church and his successor his residual legatees, and obligated them to pay all his remaining debts.

6. Collectors and Fiscal Nuncios

In the topical index to the Calendar will be found, under "collector or nuncio," a list of those officers from the pontificate of Gregory XI, and each collector has his line in the index of proper names. The chamberlain once ordered up a list of these essential functionaries of the fiscal system. The roster is to be found in Calendar no. 600: forty collectories, each identified with the man who served it at the end of 1375. Each entry is followed in the register by six or seven blank lines, so that replacements could be noted as they occurred. Few did occur. Pierre de Cros' force of collectors, mostly inherited from Arnaud Aubert, continued in office through 1378, the foundation of the Avignon political economy. There were flaws and faults in it, however, and these are most revealing. One collectory, Le Puy, is missing entirely from the 1375 list; and whether the omission was intentional or not, Le Puy was contested territory.

The former collector of Scandinavia, Pierre Gervais, ended his Cameral career as cantor of Le Puy, collector of Le Puy, Clermont, S. Flour, and Mende; these four dioceses in the north of the province of Bourges were by custom one collectory. In April 1372, old and infirm, needing help with his duties, Gervais was given at his own request Jean Dieudonné, also a canon of Le Puy and papal chaplain, as co-collector and general commissioner, beginning immediately. By an anomaly that was never solved or really clarified, the diocese of Mende was subject (as a fiscal resource) both to Gervais and to its own collector, Pierre de Montaurose. Dieudonné's commission extended to Mende as well. His letter of commission gave him the powers usually held by collectors, but it left unsettled the question of who was now responsible to the Camera for the collectory (Calendar no. 80). Montaurose remained in service at Mende, addressed as subcollector (Calendar nos. 166 and 310) but apparently still insisting on the title of collector, which was conceded to him in May and October 1375 even though the new collector of Le Puy, Vital de Bosmejo, had Mende still included in his mandate (Calendar nos. 475, 584).

The Camera continued to address Pierre Gervais as collector of Le Puy as late as February 1375 (Calendar nos. 168, 178, 414). Then, in mid-April 1375, the chamberlain wrote a letter close to the bishop and chapter, condoling the death of their colleague Gervais, and asking them to assist Jean Cabrespi in his inquiries (Calendar nos. 458, 459). The new commissioner (who had been collector of England and of the province of Reims, then special nuncio in Germany) was directed not only to uncover the goods and the still unsubmitted accounts of Pierre Gervais, but also to gather information on the activities of Dieudonné, against whom the procurator fiscal was proceeding for malfeasance and defalcation of Cameral funds (Calendar no. 460, 461). Cited to Treasury Chamber, Dieudonné died in the Curia before the end of May, and Cabrespi was warranted to take all his spoils (Calendar no. 482). Cabrespi also seized the records of Gervais, so aggressively that the collector's nephew and executor feared to assert any claim to his most valuable possessions (Calendar no. 486).

The collectors were required by their commissions to answer for their operations, in person in the Camera, every two years. By the custom of the Camera the chamberlain issued a detailed recognition and quittance after such accounts had been examined by the clerks. Punctilious observance of the rules would have given us some 240 letters of recognition from the pontificate of Gregory XI. Instead we find five in Pierre de Cros's registers, and three of those cover periods longer than two years. It is true that a few formal and punctual accounts by collectors may have been lost, but we cannot escape the impression that mostly the collectors were allowed to neglect their duty to report. They were probably concealing massive malfeasance, misfeasance, and non-feasance, extortion on the one hand and neglect, purchased with bribes, on the other. Pierre de Cros did not supervise the collectors vigilantly, and when he did reprove them it was often for an excess of zeal against his fellow prelates. He often ended such a letter (e.g., Calendar no. 344) with the warning that he wanted to hear no more complaints. It is a mark against him as a fiscal administrator that he invited his subordinates to keep him in the dark.

There are many complaints of collectors and subcollectors who misused their official powers, and little sign of effective correction by the chamberlain. The collectors and special fiscal commissioners in Bremen, Crete, and Dalmatia pursued their duties and their own profit quite out of touch with the Camera (Calendar nos. 113, 514, 610). A Limousin cardinal lost the revenue from a benefice because he used the collector of Bourges as his private transfer agent, and the collector died before paying (Calendar no. 88). The power of excommunicating to enforce Cameral claims, rashly delegated to collectors who then more even foolishly armed their subcollectors with it, intensified the effect of their local tyrannies (Calendar nos. 112, 181, 320, 418). The collector of Reims feared ipsofacto excommunication for imprisoning one of his own defalcating subcollectors (Calendar no. 333). Arnold de Verneuil, collector of Castile, complained to the Camera in 1373 that the bishop of Oviedo had attacked, beaten, and imprisoned him. The bishop, summoned to the Auditio Camere, failed to appear and the sequestration of his goods was ordered, to be carried out not by the collector but by the bishop of Astorga. But then, in 1375, the collector himself was required to appear before the chamberlain in Treasury Chamber to answer for irregularities in his accounts.[73]

---

[73] Calendar nos. 271 and 496; EFR *Grégoire XI secrètes autres*, nos. 2373 and 2870.

C. Fiscal Resources of the Apostolic See

The collectors were responsible for gathering taxes from the clergy in certain customary categories. In all of these the returns were sluggish and uncertain.[74]

1. Services

The common services were owed by custom for every appointment of a prelate, that is, an abbot or archimandrite, a bishop, archbishop, or patriarch. These payments were divided equally between the Apostolic Camera and the Camera of the College of Cardinals, hence the name "common services." The College's half was divided equally among those cardinals who were personally present in Consistory when the prelate was appointed. There were also five "minute services" paid to curial functionaries, each of the five services equal to one cardinal's share of the common services. In principle, the common services for each episcopal or monastic preferment were one-third of the real annual income of the *mensa* (as the prelate's own income base was called).[75]

In the time of Gregory XI, many of the evaluations were obsolete and some prelates tried to use that fact as an excuse to evade services. On 19 May 1373 the pope insisted that every prelate should pay common services for his provision to a bishopric or abbacy, and if the income had not been taxed at its real current value, the services should nevertheless be paid, at the customary level.[76]

2. Visitations *ad Limina* and "Census"

Bishops were obliged by custom to make a visit to the Apostolic See every two years, the *visitatio ad limina apostolorum*, making a customary offering. If the diocese paid an annual *census*, the *visitatio* was the usual occasion to pay this as well, and the total offering had come to be called *census*. The visit could be made by proxy. On 19 November 1371, Gregory XI ordered Pierre de Cros to compel all prelates, clerics, and others, whoever were in arrears, to make their *visitationes ad limina* and to pay their census and biennial procurations. He pressed again for collection of arrears of various dues in a letter of 21 February 1372. It is surpris-

---

[74] For these categories of income, the description of Samaran-Mollat, 11–68, is still standard and provides the basis for my observations. For a rapid synthesis see Jean Favier, "Finances pontificales: XIIIe-XVe siècles," in *Dictionnaire historique de la papauté* (Paris, 1994), 683–87.

[75] William E. Lunt, *Papal Revenues in the Middle Ages*, 2 vols., Records of Civilization 19 (New York, 1934), 1:85–89.

[76] EFR *Grégoire XI secrètes France*, no. 2956. I am at a loss to interpret the chamberlain's efforts to prevent the collection of any services from the abbot of Bourg-sur-Gironde (Calendar no. 479).

ing that the pope felt a need to push de Cros, since these collections were normal duties of the chamberlain and he already had all the powers necessary to carry them out.[77]

3. Subsidies

Subsidies were gifts of money extracted from the clergy beyond the customary taxes. Subsidies were claimed from the clergy to meet particular needs of the pope, especially for military operations. Usually a clerical subsidy was an income tax, a tenth or a thirtieth of the income of an ecclesiastical benefice as that income was evaluated for annates.[78] The subsidies which Pierre de Cros labored to collect included some thirtieths imposed by Clement VI and by Urban V; the revenue from these was slight.

Subsidies in France provided the occasion for the pope and the king to resolve their competing fiscal claims on the national clergy. In consideration of the royal assent, Urban V had shared with Charles V two biennial tenths in France proper, to run from 1365 through 1368, and in November 1370, shortly before he died, he decreed a third biennial tenth, this one in Languedoc, to pay for the expulsion of the free companies of brigands. Gregory XI instructed the clergy to pay their current tenths and arrears, but in response to many protests of poverty, war, and famine he halved the taxed evaluations on which the tenth was based, for all of Languedoc, imitating Urban V's example in the north.[79] He imposed a tenth of his own on Germany, Hungary, Bohemia, Poland, Sweden, and Denmark in 1372, while the last shared tenth in France was still in effect (Calendar nos. 284, 383, 406). Then, to pay the costs of the war against the Visconti, he imposed early in 1373 his own subsidy on France, the "Lingua Gallicana," and Iberia. This subsidy was not shared, and not rated on income, but imposed according to the collectors' sense of "what can be got from the clergy."[80] The chamberlain avoided using the old name for a non-rated subsidy, "caritativum" or "graciosum." He did not wish to encourage the notion that the payment was voluntary. An

---

[77] Lunt, *Papal Revenues*, 1:61–63 and 91–93; EFR *Grégoire XI secrètes France*, nos. 481 and 482; *Grégoire XI secrètes autres*, no. 556; Samaran-Mollat, 237.

[78] Lunt, *Papal Revenues*, 1:73–77, 80–81.

[79] Samaran-Mollat, 12–22.

[80] Calendar no. 567; Pierre de Cros used the phrase "de possibilitate cleri" with this meaning, writing to Bernard Cariti, collector of Sens and Rouen, 10 September 1375.

anti-Visconti subsidy was also demanded from Sicily.[81] In 1376 the pope decreed a tenth in France once again, this one to be shared with the king.[82]

Like subsidies, "tallages" were levied to meet military emergencies; but tallages were imposed by a local authority on lay as well as clerical inhabitants of a place directly threatened. The contributors were expected to pay willingly and rapidly for their own protection. So, for example, the chamberlain and Juan Fernández de Heredia, the Hospitaller castellan of Amposta, as captain general of the Comtat Venaissin, took a tallage to fight off the Breton free companies in 1375 (Calendar nos. 399, 426, 440, 443, 445, 463, 536, 548, 553, 580). Similarly, the Limousin clerics of the Curia and hierarchy were assessed a tallage for the redemption of the castles and towns of their own country (Calendar nos. 43, 580, 605).

4. Annates or "Vacancy"

Minor benefices, those subject to the authority of a bishop or abbot, owed annates or "fruits of the first year," normally one-half of one year's income. Beginning in the time of Gregory XI this charge was informally called the "vacancy" because it was the price for entering a vacant benefice; the earliest instance in the Calendar is no. 35, of 10 December 1371. The taxed value of the annates was fixed for most benefices, and the collector was able by custom to take either the taxed value or the remainder of the real income. Early in his pontificate Gregory XI demanded annates, or a tax equal to annates, from all benefices granted in his first three years.[83] At the end of the three years, the reservation of annates was extended during the pope's pleasure.[84] On 19 May 1373 he provided that even when a minor benefice was collated by a letter in common form for a poor cleric, annates should be collected as for any other collation.[85] The Camera considered annates to remain as a burden on the benefice as long as they remained unpaid. A Norfolk parish was left so burdened by Simon Sudbury when he became bishop

---

[81] BNF, MS. lat. 5913A, a collection of documents concerning the Camera and both Sicilies, includes on fols. 36r-39r an appeal to Bertrand du Mazel, nuncio in the kingdom of Sicily, dated Trapani, 1 August 1374, on his claim of arrears of subsidies. This is a Cameral copy of the appeal, once sealed close with the seal of the chamberlain and addressed to Mazel; the bow-and-arrow paper is the same as that of the chamberlain's register, Collectoriae 356.

[82] Samaran-Mollat, 56–61; Coll. 359A, 21r-22r; Calendar no. 628.

[83] *Dum incumbentia Camere*, 17 April 1371, copied into the chamberlain's dossier, Coll. 359A, 15r-16r, cited EFR *Grégoire XI secrètes autres*, no. 120 from the *Bullarium generale*.

[84] 16 April 1374: Coll. 359A, 20r-21r; abstract in EFR *Grégoire XI secrètes France*, no. 3346 from RV 266, 80v.

[85] Copied into the chamberlain's dossier, Coll. 359A, 18v; edited EFR *Grégoire XI secrètes France*, no. 2956 from RV 265, 130v.

of London (Calendar no. 109); a subdeanery of Orléans was eventually relieved of five successive arrears of annates, left unpaid by a succession of relatives of the Roger and Aubert popes (Calendar no. 100). Delays in the payment of annates had been granted quite freely in view of the impoverishment of benefices by war, famine, and plague, but at the end of 1375 all delays were revoked because of unusual burdens on the Camera, especially the impending transfer of the court to Italy (Calendar no. 594). In 1376 the pope declared all newly collated benefices liable to the payment of annates, even if the grant had not come from his own chancery.[86]

5. Visitation Procurations Reserved

When bishops and archdeacons made their annual pastoral and judicial visits to the church institutions of their dioceses, their traveling and lodging expenses were defrayed by each church with a customary payment called a procuration. Clement VI permitted bishops to collect the procurations without making the visitation, beginning the separation of this payment from its pastoral purpose. Urban V ordered bishops to collect only half their customary procurations, reserving the rest to himself. Gregory XI insisted on collecting the arrears of those half-procurations.[87] Visitation procurations were reserved anew for two years in France, Navarre, and Majorca on 19 November 1371: this was the "biennial procuration" mentioned in the chamberlain's letters; it was renewed at the end of 1375 for northern and southern France and Provence, and the chamberlain enforced it with his own order to the collectors (Calendar no. 598). The archbishops (Pierre de Cros as archbishop of Bourges among them) were instructed to forbid their suffragans and all subordinates to take the customary procurations for their visitations. Half the procurations of bishops and archbishops, and the full procurations of abbots, archdeacons, archpriests, and other canonical visitors, were reserved to the Apostolic See.[88] It must have been plain to the pope that the pastoral visitations would seldom be made by bishops and archdeacons who could take no reimbursement, but in his letters to the collectors of France, he declared that the funds were needed to combat certain sons of perdition who were inflicting damage on the lands of the Church especially in Italy: the Visconti war was the occasion.[89] In one case, an archdeacon's procurations were assigned back so that the properties of the benefice, long neglected by an absentee incumbent's proc-

---

[86] Samaran-Mollat, 23–34; Coll. 359A, 22v-23r.

[87] A survey of the visitation procurations collected from the province of Bourges in the time of Urban V: EFR *Grégoire XI secrètes France*, no. 983.

[88] RV 274, 198v: EFR *Grégoire XI secrètes France*, no. 465.

[89] *Reperiri nesciens Sathane*, as addressed to Jean Maubert, collector of Reims, ed. Samaran-Mollat, 237–39; Lunt, *Papal Revenues*, 1:107–11.

tors, could be repaired. The archdeaconry was that of Bourges, and the absentee archdeacon had been Gregory XI himself, then a cardinal (Calendar no. 640).

6. Spoils

The Camera's collection of "spoils," the movable goods and debts of deceased clerics, a practice begun in a serious way under John XXII, had become after half a century's exercise a crucially important element of the Camera's activity.[90] Over the century, until the practice was prohibited by the Council of Constance in 1417, there were about 1200 cases of spoils claimed by the Camera. About 160 of these claims belong to the pontificate of Gregory XI. There were fifty-seven cases in the plague years of 1374 and 1375, more than double the average over the century, but from 1376 to Gregory's death in March 1378, only nineteen cases.

Gregory XI concerned himself with the spoils system, trying to limit the ugliness and bitter feeling reflected in the name *spolia* and inherent in its brutal application. He did reserve the spoils of all prelates by his bull *Dudum ex certis* of 7 December 1372.[91] On the other hand, he renewed his predecessor's decision that the Camera Apostolica would not try to take the spoils of Benedictine priors when these were customarily the perquisite of their superior abbots.[92] And with the bull *Volentes ecclesiarum* of 21 August 1373, he codified the "moderation" which his predecessors had applied to the collection of spoils: the collectors should allow payments from the goods for the debts of the deceased, his funeral, and his servants' wages; and his private wealth could be used according to his testament.[93] When the deceased also left a major benefice vacant, its revenues up to the date of the next appointment, the "fruits of the vacancy," were taken by the Camera along with the spoils.[94]

Pierre de Cros began his work as chamberlain in 1371 with the pope's commission to secure the spoils of his predecessor Arnaud Aubert, then the spoils of the treasurer Gaucelme de Déaux.[95] Aubert had made such good use of the *moderatio* that none of his considerable wealth reached the Treasury; instead his executors built a fine donjon at Bassoues, property of the church of Auch and an important defense of the western frontier of the Toulousain; and in 1372, even while undertaking the expense of a force of 200 lances against the Visconti, de Cros permitted Aubert's memorial chaplains to spend 3000 florins of the spoils for rental properties to support themselves (Calendar no. 150). Gaucelme de Dé-

---

[90] Williman, *Right of Spoil*, especially the introductory chapters, 1–28.
[91] A. L. Tautù, *Acta Gregorii PP. XI (1370–1378)* (Rome, 1966), 96–97 from RV 275, 155v.
[92] Samaran-Mollat, 235.
[93] Tautù, *Acta Gregorii XI*, 164 from RV 276, 133v.
[94] Lunt, *Papal Revenues*, 1:99–101.
[95] EFR *Grégoire XI secrètes France*, nos. 259, 274, 276, 1355.

aux left comparatively little besides a stockpile of salt; his successor as treasurer and bishop of Maguelonne, Pierre de Vernols, compounded for 4000 florins and paid at least 2000.

The last year of Gregory XI was tormented by the huge debt which he owed to Louis of Anjou, and by the duke's unwillingness to concede delays of payment. In a touching confidential letter of 2 January 1378 to his treasurer at Avignon (Calendar Appendix A6) the pope fretted over the few possible sources for a palliative payment, including "the spoils of some deceased prelates, especially Pamplona, a very fat one, so they say."[96] The pope was confused or ill informed. True, Bernard Folcaud, the bishop of Pamplona, had died the previous June, and the pope himself had ordered the treasurer to secure the revenues of the vacancy, but the spoils were left for his successor to compound for, and may have paid nothing.[97] There were only two truly fat collections of spoils in the whole pontificate. Raimond de la Pradelle, archbishop of Nicosia, who had absorbed the goods of his predecessor at Nicosia, Philippe de Gaston, died in the Curia in 1375, leaving an accumulation of more than 22,000 florins, partly in safekeeping with Pierre de Monteruc, the Cardinal of Pamplona.[98] The other windfall of spoils came from Gomez Manrique, archbishop of Toledo, who also died in 1375, and whose executors compounded for 20,000 *dobles* and actually paid 15,000 in mid-May 1377.[99]

From all other spoils in the time of Gregory XI I can find no more than 43,000 florins of actual revenue, less than the services for a middling archbishopric. Pierre de Cros seems to have been lax about extracting spoils. Perhaps he was restrained by a delicacy in regard to the wealth of prelates like himself. In the early case of Guillaume Turpin, bishop of Angers, who died just before de Cros was appointed, the collector Gui de la Roche excused his poor results, reporting that some Cameral official or other had told him to collect the spoils, but that there was no formal reservation by the pope and no ad-hoc letter of commission. He had posted a proclamation on the cathedral door, he said, but gained nothing by it. In the end, the bishop had been poor, and his nephews and others had so raided his goods that the remainder was insufficient even to pay for the elementary maintenance of the buildings.[100] It is impossible to be certain how successful the collectors were in getting the goods and how honest in reporting and delivering them; and methods of evading even a keen and honest collector

---

[96] "Et de spoliis aliquorum decessorum praelatorum, praesertim Pampilonensis ut asseritur multum pingui [sic]."

[97] Greiner, "Un représentant," 200; Williman, *Right of Spoil*, 76, no. 157.

[98] Williman, *Right of Spoil*, 230, no. 1061 and 217, no. 988. Pierre de Monteruc, the cardinal vice-chancellor, had been bishop-elect of Pamplona when he was created cardinal, hence his informal title: Gane, *Chapitre de Notre-Dame*, 356, no. 458.

[99] Williman, *Right of Spoil*, 118, no. 380.

[100] Williman, *Right of Spoil*, 138, no. 507.

were widely known. Calendar no. 513 is a smooth, lawyerly demonstration of several of these. Finally, by the 1370s the right of spoil usually represented the last chance to collect money overdue for other taxes such as services, subsidies, and procurations, and the diminishing returns are an index of a general failure of the Avignon fiscal system.

3. The Ministerial Policies of Pierre de Cros

As early as the beginning of 1373, Pierre de Cros was living in a house of his own in Avignon rather than in the papal palace, where he, like his predecessors, had occupied a bedchamber just below the pope's. It is not clear whether Pierre was sharing the livrée de Mirault assigned to his brother Cardinal Jean de Cros, or living elsewhere.[1] In either case, he was asserting his status as a ministerial prelate, one who did not have to live under the eye of the pope in order to serve him loyally. Consciously or not, he was following the example of the cardinal vice-chancellor Pierre de Monteruc and showing the parity of the Camera with the Chancery. Besides his work as an administrative functionary, which was the subject of the previous section, his official competence extended to tasks in which his service was unpatterned and discretionary. These required him to scatter his attention and his efforts among simultaneous emergencies on both sides of the Alps. The manner in which his various projects overlapped and interrupted each other makes it impossible to adhere either to a topical or to a chronological order in recounting them.

A. Government of Avignon

One of Pierre de Cros' most arduous and complex tasks as chamberlain was to ensure sufficient housing in Avignon, at controlled rental prices, for the large personnel serving the pope and the Curia.[2] The pope was the secular lord of Avignon, and, especially when there was a military threat beyond the walls, his chamberlain had to avoid saddling the town with an excessive burden of economically and legally privileged inhabitants, the members of the Curia. The liveries, the enclosed compounds where the cardinals lived and each one ruled his own household — including an armed guard — as a sovereign prince, were inevitable

---

[1] The latter is more probable: see Hayez, "Les livrées avignonnaises de la période pontificale," 1 (1992): 106–7. For a book stolen from de Cros' house, and provisions for his household, see Calendar nos. 293 and 338.

[2] Michel Hayez, "Avignon sans les papes," in *Genèse et débuts du Grand Schisme d'Occident* (Paris, 1980), 143–57.

sources of friction which had to be minimized. The riot in Viterbo in 1367 was a fresh reminder of the consequences which could follow when these elements were assembled in a confined space and the urban peace was neglected.[3]

Pierre de Cros' predecessor as chamberlain, Arnaud Aubert, had administered the papal policy for Avignon through two sharp transitions, the return of Urban V to the city and the succession of Gregory XI. In order to prevent a disorderly and inflationary scramble for lodgings, in which some necessary functionaries of the Curia would be at a disadvantage, Urban V from Montefiascone forbade anyone to take a residence in Avignon without the approval of the chamberlain.[4] The ordinance proved worse than useless and the Council of Avignon asked for its revocation. Many followers of the Curia and owners of houses in Avignon, either ignorant of it or assuming that rentals previously approved would still be good, incurred excommunication by trespassing the letter of the bull. Later contestants for the same lodgings could choke the courts with litigation, claiming that the prior agreements, made by parties disabled by excommunication, were void. As soon as he was elected, Gregory XI had to facilitate the absolution of all the accidental offenders.[5]

The return of the Curia and its commercial followers, then the arrival of new strangers with the household of Gregory XI, caused many disorders, beyond the competition for lodging, which needed to be adjudicated. Confusion and evasion of justice prevailed, as one foreigner after another, summoned to the Temporal Court of the town, demurred on the ground that he was not a citizen but a courtier, subject to the Court of the Marshal of the Curia — or vice versa. On 12 August 1371 Pierre de Cros began a solution by opening a list for all the lay residents of the town who were not born in it: each would be registered once and for all as citizen or courtier. The criteria for the decision derived from another ordinance of Urban V, dated 26 March 1367, shortly before his journey to Italy. Unwilling to leave Avignon burdened with hundreds of followers of an absent Curia, residents who would be immune to the duties of citizenship, Urban had declared that anyone who remained in Avignon when the Curia departed would be thenceforth a citizen. In his *divisio* of the two classes, de Cros recognized that the bull had not been well publicized, and allowed that persons could be listed as courtiers who claimed not to have heard of the bull, provided that they had not betrayed their claim by submitting to any citizen obligation such as the

---

[3] Aubert Calendar, 43.

[4] *Cum ad civitatem*, 22 May 1370, ed. Aubert Calendar, 438, no. 868. Dykmans, "La fin du séjour," 17–53 introduces ASV Arm. XXXVII, vol. 27, 963r–978v, a small Cameral dossier, assembled in the 15th century, of documents concerning the housing of courtiers in Avignon, in the context of that bull.

[5] Calendar no. 17; Dykmans, "La fin du séjour," 27; Aubert Calendar nos. 868, 871.

wall-watch.[6] The registry, open in each of the parishes of Avignon in turn from 12 August to 1 November 1371, finally listed some 2350 courtiers and some 1450 citizens, all lay heads of households. To figure the full population of Avignon, of course, we must add to these all the heads of households born in Avignon; all the members of all those households, including servants; the members of religious houses; the secular clergy; residents in cardinals' liveries; and Jews.[7]

Pierre de Cros was the governor of Avignon for the city's lord, the pope. Like his predecessors, he swore to observe the customs and statutes of the city, receiving in return the oaths of loyalty of the residents through their syndics and bailiffs.[8] He appointed the viguiers and judges as well as the pope's procurator in the Temporal Court. In the spring of 1375, finding the Temporal Court badly managed and rife with extortion and corruption, Gregory XI dismissed all the notaries and commissioned the Cameral clerk Elie de Vodron and Pons de Jean, *licentiatus in utroque jure*, to reform it.[9] On 28 September Pierre de Cros promulgated new statutes for the Court, based on the recommendations of Pons de Jean.[10]

The Statutes of 1375 were entirely concerned with regularizing the operations of the Court, making these reliable and trustworthy. The substantive laws

---

[6] See Calendar no. 9 for Pierre de Cros' criteria for distinguishing the two classes. The *Liber divisionis* survives as RA 204, 428–507.

[7] RA 204 does not state the year of the *divisio*; adopting the mistaken date 1378 has led to misinterpretations by Guillemain, *La Cour*, 654–95, followed by Bruno Galland, *Les papes d'Avignon et la maison de Savoie (1309–1409)* (Rome, 1998), 81–87. Richard Trexler, "A Medieval Census: The *Liber divisionis*," *Mediaevalia et Humanistica* 17 (1966): 82–85 first corrected many mis-datings of the document, but *Bibliografia dell'Archivio Vaticano* 5 (1992) refers to articles by Pazstor and Esch, using two different incorrect dates.

[8] Calendar no. 258, 11 January 1373. For the Council of Avignon and syndics of the commune, see Anne-Marie Hayez, "Avignon, son seigneur et son conseil de ville au XIVe siècle," *Mémoires de l'Académie de Vaucluse*, 8e série, 6 (1997): 37–60.

[9] Calendar no. 468; EFR *Grégoire XI secrètes France*, no. 1851, edited from RV 267, 67r. Pons had been judge of the Temporal Court in 1371–1372 and 1374: Jacques Chiffoleau, *Les justices du pape* (Paris, 1984), 311.

[10] Daniel Williman, Karen Corsano, and Anne-Marie Hayez, "Les statuts de la cour temporelle d'Avignon en 1375," *Mémoires de l'Académie de Vaucluse*, 8e série, 8 (1999): 9–27. It was once assumed that the articles of the 1375 Statutes were later included unchanged in a fuller list of Statutes, issued by the next chamberlain in 1413: Joseph Girard and Pierre Pansier, *La Cour temporelle d'Avignon aux XIVme et XVme siècles* (Paris, 1909), 81–106. But the two ordinances were separated by a full and eventful generation, and each has a value independent of the other. In 1375, Pierre de Cros was providing for the operation of the Temporal Court on the eve of the departure of the Curia. In 1413 François de Conzié was using the authority of Pope John XXIII of the Pisan faction to correct abuses which seem to have become far worse in the interim. Even apart from the differences in their *arengae* and the proper names of the officers, the 45 items of 1375 are not entirely replicated among the 116 items of 1413, as Girard and Pansier supposed.

which were applied by the Temporal Court and enforced by its armed sergeants, it is clear, were well-known custom, and only two new ones needed to be mentioned, both in paragraph 7: "No one, of whatever status, may carry forbidden weapons or long knives, by day or night; and no dishonorable woman may dare wear a mantle, a houpeland,[11] or any other finery anywhere in the City."

The chamberlain undertook various tasks to improve the habitability of Avignon. He commissioned improvements to the flow of the Durançole, a diversion of Durance water from Bonpas through Avignon, for fighting fires, watering gardens, and washing footpaths (Calendar nos. 308, 327). He settled property disputes (Calendar nos. 211, 241). He ordered a survey of the pope's own domain in order to exploit it more profitably (Calendar no. 359). He supervised the collection of the gabelles which paid for the fortifications of the town (Calendar no. 495), took the orchards and vineyards of the neighborhood under Cameral protection (Calendar nos. 141, 522), and tried to secure the grain supply in time of shortage (Calendar nos. 434, 550).

In the last month before finally leaving Avignon, Gregory XI undertook provisions for the city's future good order directly rather than through his chamberlain. He reconfirmed the privileges and customs of the town of Avignon, as these were embodied in the grant of Innocent VI, 28 March 1358.[12] He granted to Cardinal Jean de Blauzac, who was to remain as vicar general of Avignon and the Comtat Venaissin, powers to interpret the statutes of the Temporal Court and to impose remedies if the *clavarius* should take unfair advantage of their obscure phrasing.[13] He granted the privilege of keeping fishing weirs in the Durançole, apparently reversing his chamberlain's plan to free its flow.[14] He renewed verbatim the bull by which Urban V had made citizens of all the courtiers remaining in Avignon after the departure of the Curia.[15] He forbade courtiers to leave Avignon without paying their bills.[16] Besides Cardinal Jean de Blauzac, there remained Cardinals Anglic Grimoard, Gilles Aycelin de Montagu, Guillaume de Chanac, Pierre de Monteruc the vice-chancellor, and Hugues de S. Martial. The residential compounds of the departing cardinals had their gates

---

[11] A marginal note indicates that mention of the houpeland (a long fitted dress of wool broadcloth) was taken out of the statute on 28 September 1378.

[12] Bull of 23 August 1376, *Dum Romana Ecclesia matre nostra*; Avignon, BM, MS. 2399, fols. 324r-327r is a copy in the town cartulary.

[13] Paul Achard and Léopold Duhamel, *Inventaire sommaire des Archives communales d'Avignon* (Avignon, 1863–1953), 38: archives municipales, boîte 10, 1 and 2; Archives de Vaucluse, Pintat 11/382; I owe this note to Patrick Zutshi.

[14] Avignon BM 2465, fol. 26r.

[15] RV 288, 339v; Archives de Vaucluse, Pintat 18/572.

[16] Dykmans, "La fin du séjour," 33.

and the cardinals' painted arms removed; open to the public street, they ceased to exist as liveries.[17]

B. Holy Thursday Anathema

As chamberlain, Pierre de Cros was a vigorous prosecutor of the Holy Thursday (*Coena Domini*) bull beginning *Excommunicamus et anathematizamus*, an annual proclamation by the pope of anathemas against violators of the dignity and traditional privileges of the Apostolic See.[18] Urban V had standardized the excommunication of eight classes of offenders and reinstated the practice of posting the bull on the doors of the Avignon cathedral of Notre-Dame-des-Doms.[19] Gregory XI adopted Urban V's text of the Holy Thursday bull, only adding one new class of evildoers (the eighth in the following list).[20] Gregory's *excommunicandi* were: 1) heretics; 2) pirates; 3) those who impose new tolls in their territories; 4) who carry horses, arms, steel, timber, or other contraband to the Saracens; 5) who falsify apostolic letters; 6) who harm or hinder any persons going to or returning from the Apostolic See, or who impede the supply of necessities to the Roman Curia; 7) who harm persons with causes or business in the Curia; 8) who harm or hinder pilgrims to Rome; 9) who occupy the cities, castles, towns, lands, and rights of the Roman Church, including the Comtat Venaissin and Avignon.

In his first year as chamberlain, Pierre de Cros showed a keen sensitivity to certain problems which the Holy Thursday anathemas confronted. He got the pope's letters bidding the dukes of Bourbon and Berry and their officers to protect the clergy of his diocese of Bourges and all travelers to the ecclesiastical courts of the city.[21] The Camera dispatched its own letters by couriers who reported to the chamberlain, and by other reliable carriers, usually persons with

---

[17] Michel Hayez, "Avignon sans les papes," 150.

[18] For the history of the Holy Thursday anathemas and the practice especially during the Western Schism, see Emil Göller, *Die päpstlichen Pönitentiarie*, vol. 1, part 1 (Rome, 1907), 242–77.

[19] Urban V's annual issues of *Excommunicamus et anathematizamus* are cited in EFR *Urbain V secrètes France*, nos. 343, 1689, 2174, and 3062, the last of these dated Rome, 11 April 1370; the bull of 10 April 1365 is edited at no. 1689.

[20] The text as of 25 March 1372 is in *Bullarum, diplomatum et privilegiorum sanctorum Romanorum Pontificum Taurinensis editio*, vol. 4 (Turin, 1859), 539–41, and in EFR *Grégoire XI secrètes France*, no. 731; EFR *Grégoire XI secrètes autres*, no. 3781 cites the bull as of 10 April 1376, and the *Schedario Baumgarten* notes it in the *Bullarium generale* II, c. 53.

[21] 8 February 1373: EFR *Grégoire XI secrètes France*, nos. 1089–1092.

business in the various lawcourts of the Curia, and *Coena Domini* was the law which guarded the mail.[22]

De Cros was enraged when (Calendar no. 27) some men of Mondragon, a castle belonging to the archbishop of Arles on the road east of Pont S. Esprit, demanded toll from a papal sergeant-at-arms and arrested him violently, contemptuous of his papal insignia and the bulls which he was carrying. They unhanded the sergeant only when he showed imperial bulls from his pouch. Although the chamberlain did not mention the *Coena Domini* excommunications on that occasion, he did summon the offenders to his own court of Treasury Chamber. Later (Calendar no. 342) he empowered all papal couriers and the officials of crucial dioceses to issue citations to the Camera under pain of excommunication, citations which these officials could use against any toll-takers who overstepped their authority as had those of Mondragon.

Near Montesquieu-Volvestre in the diocese of Rieux, toward the end of 1371 (Calendar no. 207), a mountain gang waylaid and robbed a group of clerics and laymen, including two knights, who were on their way to the Curia at Avignon. Acting in accordance with item 6 of the Holy Thursday anathemas, the chamberlain prosecuted the robbers with sentences of excommunication and placed Montesquieu under interdict. A similar case in the neighborhood of Oloron (Calendar no. 538) was similarly treated in 1375.

In 1375, when the pope and chamberlain needed to take action against brigands who had invaded the Comtat Venaissin, they did so (Calendar no. 416) on the basis provided by *Coena Domini*, that the brigands were hindering travel to the Apostolic See.[23]

The fullest statement of the law against trade with the Moslem enemy was constitution 71 of the Fourth Lateran Council (1215), *Ad liberandam terram sanctam*, codified in the Decretals 5.6.17.[24] This canon, which was to be proclaimed in the churches of every maritime city on Sundays and feast days, excommunicated any Christians who carried to the Saracens arms, steel, or ship-timbers, who sold them galleys or ships, or who piloted their ships or otherwise helped them in war against the Christians of the Holy Land; offenders were to be punished by the confiscation of their goods and enslavement to whoever informed on them. One confessing this crime on his deathbed could not have absolution without giving double his profit from such trade as a subsidy to the

---

[22] Two registers of the dispatch of letters are detailed in an Appendix C on the enclosed compact disk.

[23] The excommunication of the Visconti in 1373 and the famous interdict of Florence in 1376 were embodied in bulls which, as published, make no mention of these anathemas, even though the crimes charged in both instances included offenses condemned by the Holy Thursday bull.

[24] *Corpus iuris canonici*, ed. Emil Friedberg, 2 vols. (Leipzig, 1879–1881; repr. Graz, 1955), 2: col. 777.

Crusade. Such "Alexandria legacies" were a source of revenue to the Camera still under Pierre de Cros (Calendar no. 1), and he had to intervene in cases where merchandise had been confiscated by unofficial vigilantes abetted and justified by *Ad liberandam* (Calendar nos. 545, 586).

C. War Policy

Gregory XI continued the Christmas custom, apparently begun by his immediate predecessor Urban V, of presenting a blessed sword with its scabbard and a hat embroidered with pearls to an outstanding military champion of the Roman Church, for example Louis duke of Anjou who, as the French king's lieutenant in Languedoc, protected the approaches to Avignon from the west.[25] The ceremony was nothing like an act of surrender; but in a true sense the pope was a prisoner of the Hundred Years' War from his Christmas coronation until his death. The chamberlain Pierre de Cros had to manage his share of the details in financing and directing the military policy which absorbed the attention and resources of the Apostolic See.

According to Froissart,[26] when Edward Prince of Wales and of Aquitaine fell ill after the campaign of Nájera, cities of Aquitaine began to secede from English control, encouraged by the treasonous preaching of the archbishop of Toulouse, whose brother was bishop of Cahors.[27] The Prince considered himself betrayed and swore vengeance. By the treaty of Brétigny, 6 May 1360, an English garrison had occupied the castle of Limoges. The bishop Jean de Cros seemed to be on excellent terms with the Black Prince,[28] but on 22 August 1370 he received the dukes of Berry and Bourbon for a two-day visit in the cité of Limoges (the bishop's precinct, containing the cathedral and the castle) with an army corps of 1200 lances and 3000 footsoldiers. Departing, the dukes left the castle

---

[25] VQ 6:357 and 386 for Christmas 1370 and 1371, when the sword and cap went to Louis of Anjou; also Eugène Müntz, "Les épées d'honneur distribuées par les papes pendant les XIVe, XVe et XVIe siècles," *Revue de l'art chrétien* 39 (1889): 408–11. Pierre de Cros' sword "Archiepiscopus," described above, was likely such a ceremonial gift.

[26] Froissart, *Chroniques*, ed. Kervyn van Lettenhove (Brussels, 1867–1877), 7:338–41; trans. Berners 2:268–70, chap. 252. See Denifle, *La désolation des églises, monastères et hopitaux en France pendant la Guerre de Cent Ans*, 2:558–62 for a good strategic account of the campaign with notes of the chronicle evidence.

[27] At the date in question, however, the archbishop of Toulouse was Geoffroi de Veyrols (1361–1376) and the bishop of Cahors was her native son Bego de Castelnau (1366–1388). Froissart was possibly thinking of the brothers Pierre de la Jugie, archbishop of Narbonne (1347–1375) and Hugues de la Jugie, bishop of Carcassonne (1371), nephews of Clement VI.

[28] Evidence in Guillaume Mollat, "Cros (Jean de)," *DHGE* 13 (1956), cols. 1064–65.

under the flag of France with a garrison of 100 lances, enough to continue the provocation of Prince Edward without seriously protecting the Cité. He marched his army from Bordeaux to Limoges, his miners sapped the wall of the Cité, and on 19 September a section fell in. According to Froissart, three noble captains, Jean de Villemur, Jean de la Roche, and the squire Roger de Beaufort, stood in the breach and challenged all comers. The duke of Lancaster, the earl of Cambridge, and the earl of Pembroke assailed the three French captains and captured them.[29] The cité of Limoges was sacked and Edward threatened the bishop Jean de Cros with death, but John of Gaunt, duke of Lancaster, ransomed him to the king of France for 100 francs in February 1371. He went to the court at Avignon where his cousin Pierre Roger de Beaufort had just been elected pope.[30] Jean de Cros became Cardinal of Limoges on 30 May 1371, and his brother Pierre de Cros was appointed papal chamberlain on 20 June. Then the pope sent a whole pouch of letters to the English who had taken possession of the bishop's properties, calling on them to behave with justice and mercy. In particular he asked Edmund of Langley, earl of Cambridge, to restore castles and lands which belonged to Jean de Cros. A similar flurry of protective letters, to both to the English and the French territorial lords, went out on behalf of Pierre de Cros early in 1372 and again in 1373.[31]

Roger de Beaufort was the brother and Jean de la Roche the nephew of the pope-to-be Pierre Roger de Beaufort; Jean de Villemur was related to Pons de Villemur the bishop of Couserans; and all three captains had served in the French army.[32] Through his whole pontificate Gregory XI worked without success to get Roger de Beaufort released. He asked Bertrand du Guesclin to exchange one of his English prisoners to Jean de Grailly the Captal de Buch, Roger's captor; he wrote to the Black Prince and to Joan of Kent, John of Gaunt, Edmund of Langley, Alice Perrers, and Louis of Anjou for help in negotiating the extortionate ransom set by the Captal. He used his brother-in-law and master of his household Hugues de la Roche to plead for Jean and Roger together. Roger was married by proxy to Jeanne de Rais, who was willing but unable to ransom him. He was inherited as a prisoner by a new Captal, and Gregory's final efforts with Richard II of England to arrange a ransom remained fruitless.[33]

---

[29] Froissart, *Chroniques*, ed. Kervyn, 8:38–43; trans. Berners, 2:355–57, chap. 283.

[30] EFR *Grégoire XI secrètes France*, no. 32; and see Anne-Lise Rey-Courtel, "Les cardinaux du Midi pendant le Grand Schisme," in *Le Midi et le Grand Schisme d'Occident* (Toulouse, 2004), 49–118, here 54–55.

[31] EFR *Grégoire XI secrètes France*, nos. 142–47, 573–76, and 1089–92.

[32] Froissart, *Chroniques*, ed. Kervyn, 7:339, 7:464, and 8:7; trans. Berners, 2:268–70, chap. 252.

[33] Guillemain, *La Cour*, 172–73 and Paul R. Thibault, *Pope Gregory XI* (Lanham, MD, 1986), 206–7 assemble the documentation: EFR *Grégoire XI secrètes France*, nos. 183, 405, 1866, 1844, 1845, 417, 418, 413, 504–9, 1028, 2063.

The English and their allies clearly wanted to keep Roger and la Roche prisoners as a reminder to the pope that they considered him French in interest, not neutral. By the circumstances which surrounded his election and by the interests of the personnel of his Curia, Pope Gregory XI was committed to the well-being of the Limousin and deeply implicated in the war policies of the French crown. Whatever a neutral papacy might have done to sedate the Hundred Years' War, his papacy could not do. His paternal letters in 1371 advising restraint on both sides were ignored, and both the English and the French used the pope's truce of Bruges, begun in 1375 and renewed until midsummer 1377, only for posturing and strategic rest.[34] Furthermore, the infection of the war spread to the papal domains.

The Breton soldiers whose savagery eventually blighted Gregory's last months and blotted his memory first came into the Limousin as an army of 200 lances under the command of Bertrand du Guesclin, lately a brigand captain in the Comtat Venaissin.[35] They took from the English S. Yrieix and other important towns and castles. When du Guesclin was appointed marshal of France, he left the Bretons in garrison of those places. An early notice of the Breton commander Silvestre Budes, related by marriage to du Guesclin, is as captain of the garrison of S. Macaire.

Gregory XI's project of redeeming castles of the Limousin by contributions from Limousin clerics is marked by a letter of 29 June 1373.[36] The pope was aiming at a relatively modest sum, 1900 fl., to be raised from clerics and laity of Limousin origin residing in the Curia at Avignon. The commissioners, who were to distribute the burden of the subsidy, were Faydit d'Aigrefeuille, bishop of Avignon, and Maurice de la Barde, clerk of the Camera, for the clergy; and for the laity the squires Pierre Lefèvre, Bertrand de Veyrac, and Raoul de Lestranges. The English garrisons had in some cases surrendered or sold out to Breton soldiers, who were now demanding a price for their peaceful departure. The chamberlain extended the scope of the appeal, pressing all ecclesiastical dignitaries of

---

[34] R. Delachenal, ed., *Chronique des règnes de Jean II et de Charles V* (Paris, 1910–1920), 2:176–81; Richard G. Davies, "The Anglo-papal Concordat of Bruges, 1375: A Reconsideration," *Archivum historiae pontificiae* 19 (1981): 97–146.

[35] Froissart, *Chroniques*, ed. Kervyn, 8:36–38; trans. Berners, 2:354–58, chap. 282. The rise of the Free Companies after the Treaty of Brétigny is explained by Kenneth Fowler, *Medieval Mercenaries* 1: *The Great Companies* (Oxford, 2001), esp. chap. 1, "Dramatis Personae," for the captains Bertrand and Olivier du Guesclin, Silvestre Budes, Jean de Malestroit, Bernard de la Salle, and John Hawkwood. Their wars in Italy are to be the subject of *Medieval Mercenaries* 2.

[36] Guillemain, *La Cour*, 612, nn. 202–3; the letter is noted in EFR *Grégoire XI secrètes France*, no. 1260 and transcribed in Calendar Appendix A3 on the enclosed compact disk.

Limousin origin, not only in Avignon but wherever they were living, to give to the patriotic cause.[37]

Brigand gangs, mostly Breton veterans of the campaign against the Black Prince, crossed the Rhône into the Comtat Venaissin in December 1373, led by Silvestre Budes and Olivier du Guesclin the brother of the constable of France.[38] The rector of the Comtat, Aymar de Poitiers, the pope's brother-in-law, count of Valentinois, took wartime wages until he died on 2 June.[39] Pierre de Cros then kept the title and wages of the rector in his own hands until his departure for Italy in 1376, while a deputy, Jean de Cheylard, prior of Charay, saw to the judicial functions of the office.[40] In June 1374 the pope declared the brigands excommunicated and appointed Juan Fernández de Heredia (castellan of Amposta and rival of Raimond Béranger for mastership of the Hospitallers) captain-general of the Comtat Venaissin. Heredia took a tallage from the inhabitants and improved the fortifications of the province. The Estates of Provence also had to vote a tallage.[41] The Gascon captain Bernard de la Salle, under contract to the pope but not needed in Lombardy, applied military pressure to the Bretons. The pope intensified his excommunication, the chamberlain published it throughout the province and summoned the pope's vassals to their duty. After a year of costly guerilla war the Bretons, reduced to terrorizing for bread, took a ransom, gave hostages, and temporarily withdrew.[42] As soon as they were gone, de Cros thriftily dismissed the guard troops, all but la Salle's.[43]

A fresh nuisance had already begun in the Comtat, the criminal course of Bertrand des Baux. At Vacqueyras, on the plain below Montmirail, 26 kilometers northeast of Avignon, he and his accomplices captured and killed Dondino da Pescara, a former judge of the Temporal Court and of the Bishop's Court of Avignon (Calendar nos. 428, 446). Summoned to trial in the Rector's Court of the Comtat Venaissin, Bertrand first got pardons for his accomplices, then went on a rampage of murder and abduction, occupying Gigondas, a safer base further up the mountain. But a small force from the palace guard carried siege machinery

---

[37] EFR *Grégoire XI secrètes France*, nos. 2634, 1393, and 1822; the last is the pope's commission to Pierre de Cros for this project, edited below in Appendix A3 on the enclosed compact disk.

[38] Segrè, ed., "I dispacci," 61 and 66; Robert André-Michel, "La défense d'Avignon sous Urbain V et Grégoire XI," *Mélanges* 30 (1910): 129–45.

[39] The regular wage of the rector was already quite handsome, £2 Tours per day; on 23 March it rose to £7.13.5: Claude Faure, *Etude sur l'administration et l'histoire du Comtat-Venaissin du XIIIe au XVe siècle (1229–1417)* (Paris and Avignon, 1909), 51 and 151–53.

[40] Calendar no. 428; Faure, *Etude*, 214; Chevalier, *Bio-Bibliographie,* 1:1075.

[41] Calendar nos. 399, 548.

[42] Calendar nos. 416, 441, 444, 494; EFR *Grégoire XI secrètes France*, no. 1372; Faure, *Etude*, 152–53.

[43] Calendar nos. 534, 536.

and heavy arbalests up the Ouvèze on barges. Compelled to surrender, Bertrand was imprisoned, comfortably, in the palace at Avignon on 6 July 1375. It may be that his felonies were found pardonable as the excesses and mistakes of an ally in the war against the Breton brigands; in any case he had been freed before the following April.[44]

The Bretons, meanwhile, had been troubling Provence, even burning the winter wheat before it could be harvested in 1375. The Estates, with the chamberlain and Cardinal Pierre d'Estaing as intermediaries, offered a tribute for their departure.[45] The next spring they returned to the Comtat Venaissin, gathered in companies under Jean de Malestroit and Silvestre Budes. The guard force of Bernard de la Salle, their adversary a year earlier, had gone off in October to garrison the legate's forts in Perugia. It made sense now to hire the Bretons for use in Italy against the rebellious cities and their sponsor Florence.

When the Curia and Pierre de Cros left Avignon, his successor as rector of the Comtat Venaissin was the pope's brother Guillaume de Beaufort, viscount of Turenne. Appointed 2 October 1376, for more than two years he had been keeping the military chest for the pope, lending money to the treasurer of the Comtat Venaissin against future revenue from the tallage.

The brigandage in the neighborhood of Avignon was dangerous and costly to the papal power, but the long Visconti war in Italy was far worse. Success had seemed almost within reach in the long struggle against the brothers Bernabò and Galeazzo Visconti when Gregory XI was crowned at the beginning of 1371. Cardinal Pierre d'Estaing, who had undertaken the government of Perugia in 1370, went to Bologna as Gregory's legate responsible for the Romagna. His receiver or treasurer general in Italy from April 1371 to the end of 1375 was Bernard de Bonval, bishop of Spoleto and then of Bologna.[46] In July 1371 Cardinal Philippe Cabassole occupied Perugia with a legatine commission for the southern provinces of the Church state. The pope hoped that the two cardinal legates together could finish the work of the great Gil Albornoz, creating a single Church State with one system of laws, weights, measures, and coinage.[47]

With Bologna and the Patrimony ready to bear the burdens of their own defense, and with a new "Guelph League" sealed at Florence against the Visconti,[48] Pierre de Cros undertook offensive alliances in the north. Early in 1372 he began

---

[44] Faure, *Etude*, 153–54.
[45] Calendar no. 553.
[46] EFR *Grégoire XI secrètes autres*, nos. 115, 249.
[47] *Prima Vita Gregorii XI* in Baluze-Mollat 1:417–18. Cf. Theiner 2:542–47, nos. 531, 533, 538, and 539 for instructions to the cardinal legates. Philippe Cabassole's appointment was dated 4 July 1371: copy in Viterbo, Biblioteca comunale, pergamene sciolte no. 608.
[48] On 24 October 1371: Giuliano Lucarelli, *I Visconti di Milano e Lucca* (Lucca, 1984), 39–41.

assembling the Church's contingent for the Guelph League, renegotiating previous contracts with the count of Landau.[49] In July the pope commissioned de Cros to form a league with Amadeo VI the "Green Count" of Savoy, Secondotto marquis of Montferrat, and Otto duke of Brunswick.[50] Gregory XI hoped that one of his military vicars would assume leadership of the league's forces, but he was disappointed. Galeazzo Malatesta, vicar of Rimini, was approached first, then Gomez Albornoz, knight of Cuenca, vicar of Ascoli, who had led an earlier Church-league army to victory against Ambrosio Visconti at Sacco del Tronto in 1366.[51] When the captain-general of Niccolò, marquis d'Este and vicar of Ferrara, also failed to step forward, the pope pointedly reminded Cardinal d'Estaing that 10,000 florins were due in census for that vicariate.[52] Pierre de Cros sent the archdeacon of Paphos to enlist a Church contingent of 200 lances in Aquitaine (Calendar nos. 149, 151). Bernabò Visconti had called a truce and offered terms of peace in mid-1372 but, fearing to be fooled again by strategic delay, the pope himself temporized, sending Bernabò's letter back to Italy for Pierre d'Estaing to review.[53]

Meanwhile, on 27 August 1372, Philippe Cabassole died at Perugia. Gerald du Puy, abbot of Marmoutiers, was there already with the title of receiver general.[54] On 9 September he was promoted vicar general in Cabassole's place, expected to occupy Perugia and Orvieto and to watch and exploit the Patrimony of S. Peter in Tuscany.[55] The abbot energetically pushed to completion the two fortresses begun in Perugia by Pierre d'Estaing. These were located at the two ends of the present Corso Bersaglieri, one incorporating the Porta S. Antonio and the other on the mound of the Porta Sole. Between the two he had a roofed corridor built, on arches where it did not follow the city wall, so that one garrison could assist the other. Then he extended the corridor to the Palazzo dei Priori, which he had appropriated, as an escape route for himself, even thrusting it through the wall of the cathedral near the high altar. The works cost, it was said, 240,000 florins.[56] Du Puy was further expected to raise a staggering 4000 fl. each month

---

[49] The contracts had originally been made by Guillaume Gascon, bishop of Siena, formerly bishop of Comacchio: EFR *Grégoire XI secrètes France*, no. 2459.

[50] A copy of the treaty of alliance was dispatched together with a letter of the chamberlain on 27 July 1372: Calendar Appendix C1 on the enclosed compact disk.

[51] Theiner 2:539, no. 528; EFR *Grégoire XI secrètes autres*, no. 664.

[52] Theiner 2:539–46, nos. 530, 535, and 537.

[53] Theiner 2:548, no. 544.

[54] The abbot was in the Curia at the beginning of the pontificate, and associated with Pierre de Cros: Hoberg, *Inventare*, 496. Italian sources often refer to him as "abbate di Monmaggiore," a more famous monastery.

[55] EFR *Grégoire XI secrètes autres*, no. 988; copy in Viterbo, Biblioteca comunale, pergamene sciolte no. 608.

[56] The story of Gerald du Puy in Perugia is elegantly told by Luigi Bonazzi, *Storia di Perugia dalle origine al 1860* (Perugia, 1875), 1:432–87. More laborious, but with the

from the southern Papal States.[57] The round sum of gold was the amount needed to pay 200 lances under contract, probably John Hawkwood's soldiers, who had supported Perugia's rebellion in 1369 but who had now gone over to the Church and were being directed by Pierre d'Estaing in Lombardy.

An offer of concerted action by the emperor Charles IV in the summer of 1372 persuaded the pope to resume a hard line against the Visconti. On 3 August 1372, finding Bernabò and Galeazzo Visconti guilty in absentia of lese majesty and the violation of the Church's lands and rights, Charles IV finally withdrew his authority from them, depriving them of their vicariates and of all other imperial titles, and placing them under the ban of the Empire. There were two formal sentences against each, four imperial bulls in all. In a letter of the same date to the pope, Charles IV set aside his imperial interest in the lands and cities which Bernabò had taken in the last ten years; the Church could take them, or could grant them to a promising supporter. The pope arranged to make the count of Savoy his own avenging champion and the emperor's vicar by altering the terms of Pierre de Cros' alliance with him: now Amadeo was not obliged to restore to Queen Joan of Naples any recovered lands which had been Angevin.[58] The emperor then obligingly made Amadeo his vicar.[59] The imperial sentences against Bernabò were wanted to justify and abet the rebellion of towns subject to him. They could not be proclaimed in Milan, of course, but they were sent to Lucca and published there, and Pierre de Cros made ready to have them cried and posted in several cities, contained within his own letter-patent of 11 October.[60]

In his dispatch to Mantua at Christmas 1372 Cristoforo Tolomei reported the pope enraged and committed to war against the Visconti.[61] Rumor was that the pope's brother Guillaume, viscount of Turenne, would lead 2000 lances into Italy and that 300 lances were already on their way to Bologna. These would be the forces enlisted by the viscount's brother Nicolas and son Raimond de Turenne, with Guillaume de Lordat, the bishop of Lucca and war treasurer in Piedmont and Lombardy.[62] The pope was expected to condemn the Visconti

---

advantage of photographs and a map, Eugenio Duprè Theseider, "La rivolta di Perugia nel 1375 contro l'abate di Monmaggiore [sic] ed i suoi precedenti politici," *Bolletino della Reale deputazione di storia patria per l'Umbria* 35 (1938): 69–166.

[57] Theiner 2, nos. 541, 552, 554.

[58] EFR *Grégoire XI secrètes France*, nos. 2600, 2690 (also ed. Theiner 2:549, no. 547), 3218, 3219, 3329; EFR *Grégoire XI secrètes autres*, nos. 1363 and 1363bis.

[59] 23 November 1372: Theodor Sickel, "Das Vicariat der Visconti," *Sitzungsberichte der Kaiserlichen Akademie der Wissenschaften*, Philosophisch-historische Klasse, 30.1 (1859): 3–90, here 38–41.

[60] See Calendar nos. 183, 185, and 186; Lucarelli, *I Visconti di Milano e Lucca*, 41.

[61] Segrè, ed., "I dispacci," 42.

[62] Jean Glénisson, "Les origines de la révolte de l'Etat pontifical en 1375," *Rivista di Storia della Chiesa in Italia* 5 (1951): 145–68, here 156. Raimond de Turenne had taken a

for heresy at the next Consistory (7 January 1373), and then to crush them with a Crusade. Three emissaries of Galeazzo Visconti whom Cristoforo named as present in the Curia were granted a safe-conduct by the chamberlain (Calendar no. 249); but they were wanted, not to discuss peace, but to carry back the papal bull summoning the Visconti brothers to hear their sentence on 28 March.

While the canonical term of three warnings to the Visconti was running, Gregory XI did not wait for their repentance, but assembled a military staff and gathered money to pay for a definitive victory in Lombardy. Cristoforo Tolomei's dispatch of 22 February 1373 summarizes the grand effort.[63] A rated subsidy everywhere but in Italy was to raise 3 million florins: prelates were to pay a quarter of annual incomes over 1000 florins, or a tenth of lesser incomes, each year for the duration of the war. Cardinals, prelates, and scribes in the Curia gave almost 200 thousand florins and pledged more.[64] Certain officials, including the chamberlain, were charged with specific business of the war. Two wronged and vengeful Visconti joined the army. The bishop of Vercelli and the viscount of Turenne were to command it. The bishop intended to take Vercelli back by force from Galeazzo Visconti. The viscount could expect a part of the territorial spoils, and in fact the emperor granted him Chiusi.[65]

The surviving registers of Pierre de Cros' letters show him active in two of the joint efforts for the war in Lombardy, using pawns from the Treasury to borrow money and directing the work of the collectors gathering the subsidies outside the Curia. The generous donations at Avignon, however, were not in his hands, and he had no role in the military operations. Similarly, the general inquest of 1373 into the condition and wealth of the Order of the Hospital, which would normally have been directed from the Camera, escaped his control.[66] Gregory XI did not truly lead or even shape his curial administration, and he had no sense of a cabinet of department heads with well-defined competencies.

---

loan of 451 francs from the company of Antonius Pauli of Florence, and the chamberlain registered this as a debt owed by the Camera on 20 May 1372: VQ 6:392.

[63] Segrè, ed., "I dispacci," 44–50.

[64] The archbishops of Narbonne (Pierre de la Jugie), Rouen (Philippe d'Alençon), and Nicosia (Raimond de la Pradelle) were particularly generous. Cristoforo guessed that Raimond was in the Curia seeking a red hat, but he died in 1376 still archbishop of Nicosia. Philippe d'Alençon did not get promotion from Gregory XI; adhering to Urban VI in 1378, he was one of 25 cardinals in the first creation of the Roman sect. Gregory XI did make his cousin Pierre de la Jugie cardinal in 1375.

[65] The grant, dated 8 September 1378, was registered with the Camera Apostolica by the viscount's proctor Luigi di Monticolo: Perugia, Archivio di Stato, Bolle, breve e diplomi, cassetto 9, 183 and 184.

[66] See the introduction by Anthony Luttrell to Jean Glénisson, ed., *L'enquête pontificale de 1373 sur l'Ordre des Hospitaliers de S-Jean de Jérusalem*, 1: A.-M. Legras and R. Favreau, *L'enquête dans le Prieuré de France* (Paris, 1987).

He seems to have assigned tasks haphazardly, to whichever of his servants was at hand when an emergency arose.

Bernabò and Galeazzo Visconti incurred excommunication when they failed to obey the pope's summons to his Consistory of 28 March 1373. The victory of Enguerrand de Coucy and John Hawkwood for the Church at Montechiari on 7 May caused a military standoff. Taking advantage of the emperor's license, the pope in June appointed an imperial vicar of Voghera, Agostino Bozarelli, who was to collect the revenues of that vicariate instead of the deprived, banned, and excommunicated Galeazzo Visconti.[67]

But that summer the effort of Amadeo of Savoy suddenly went slack. The likely reason was that the war funds from the papal Treasury, destined to pay his troops, had fallen instead into the hands of his enemy. Pietro Gazata, the contemporary chronicler of Reggio Emilia, tells the surprising story immediately after his account of the Montechiari campaign:[68]

> The count of Savoy was then with his great army in the territory of Milan. It happened that month that a certain bishop, a nephew of the Roman pontiff, went to Milan under pretense of peace and offered his services, to go to the pope and negotiate a peace. He received letters from the Visconti to go and return to them in safety. When he returned to Pavia he was graciously received by Lord Galeazzo, and he told him the pope's answer; but said that he wished to go on to the count of Savoy on this business. The cautious Lord Galeazzo had inquiries made with all the bishop's men, about

---

[67] RA 173, 62v-63r, edited in Calendar Appendix A1 on the enclosed compact disk.

[68] *Chronicon Regiense ab anno MCCLXXII usque ad MCCCLXXXVIII,* auctoribus Sagaccio et Petro de Gazata Regiensibus, nunc primum editum ex manuscripto codice Bibliothecae Estensis, Rerum Italicarum Scriptores 18 (Milan, 1731), col. 80 C-D. Pietro Gazata, the continuator of this chronicle, was abbot of San Prospero in Reggio Emilia, about 39 years old at the time of the incident, and later a subcollector for Urban VI. In his preface (p. 1) Muratori praises the work for its simplicity, sincerity, and judicious accuracy. He found the chronicle incomplete, in a mouse-eaten and rotting manuscript, in the monastery where it had been written; it has not appeared in the new edition of RIS. The translation is mine; here is the Latin text: "Et tunc Comes Sabaudiae cum suo magno exercitu erat in territorio Mediolani. Evenit isto mense, quod quidam Episcopus Nepos Romani Pontificis ivit Mediolanum sub dissimulatione pacis, obtulitque se iturum ad Papam ad tractandam pacem, qui accepit literas a Vicecomitibus posse ire, et redire tute ad ipsos. Cum autem reversus fuit Papiam, receptus est gratanter a D. Galeazio, et dixit responsum Papae; sed dixit, se velle ire ad Comitem Sabaudiae pro hac causa, quem caute D. Galeatius fecit perquiri cum omnibus suis, qui erant numero quinquaginta, invenitque eum habentem centum millia ducatorum, quos ferebat ad Comitem Sabaudiae pro pagis mille lancearum pro quinque mensibus. Et hanc pecuniam habuit D. Galeatius, dimissoque Episcopo, dixit ut tute iret, quia sic ei promiserat, sed tamen non debebat ferre subsidium suis inimicis."

fifty in number, and found that he had a hundred thousand ducats which he was carrying to the count of Savoy as the pay of a thousand lances for five months. Lord Galeazzo took possession of the money and dismissed the bishop, saying that he might go safely because he had so promised, but that he should not carry subsidy to his enemies.

Gazata's account is striking and convincing, but not quite coherent. He does not explain why the pseudo-peacemaker went to Bernabò's Milan instead of Galeazzo's Pavia; and Gregory XI had no nephew who was a bishop; and the events related by Gazata, though they ended "that month" (May 1373, after Montechiari), had to have begun some time earlier. Clarification is provided by a letter of 21 March from Bernabò Visconti to Ludovico Gonzaga. Bernabò told his ally that his brother Galeazzo had been engaged in serious peace talks with Amadeo of Savoy, and that the pope's *brother-in-law* Hugues de la Roche, captain of the Church army, traveling with Amanieu de Pomiers, had asked for safe-conduct over the forty miles from Castel S. Giovanni in the territory of Piacenza to Amadeo's camp at Vimercate, crossing the lands of Pavia, then of Milan. On their return, they urged Bernabò to join their peace effort by sending a reverent embassy to the pope, a proposal that he was seriously considering. In his letter Bernabò remarked that Amadeo's forces were short of food and not making much war.[69] Under fresh safeconducts, Hugues de la Roche traveled to Avignon and returned with an armed escort and the gold so desperately needed by Amadeo and so deftly lifted by Galeazzo.[70]

If his army was not to be paid, the Green Count's heart was no longer in the fight.[71] He withdrew to the country around Bologna where his men foraged on Church land. His representatives joined those of the Visconti at Avignon late in 1373 arguing for a long truce and final peace. The shock of losing so much

---

[69] Luigi Osio, ed., *Documenti diplomatici tratti dagli archivi milanesi* 1 (Milan, 1864), no. 94, pp. 160–61.

[70] The 50 men of the escort would each have had about 15 pounds or 7 kilos of gold coin. Their leader on the return to Pavia could have been another official of the Church forces, such as Bernard de Bonval, bishop of Bologna and receiver general in the north. Pierre de Cros, the pope's cousin, addressed Bonval as cousin (Calendar no. 74), and such a distant relation might be the source of Gazata's "Nepos Episcopus."

[71] Bruno Galland gives an account of the league against the Visconti from Savoy's point of view in *Les papes d'Avignon et la maison de Savoie*, 282–97, and more particularly in "Le rôle du comte de Savoie dans la 'ligue' de Grégoire XI contre les Visconti (1372–1375)," *Mélanges* 105 (1993): 763–823. At p. 796, n. 156 he discounts the story of the Reggio chronicle: "Pour embellir encore cette anecdote, le chroniqueur n'a pas craint d'exagérer le montant de la somme interceptée: 100 000 ducats, soit le payement de 1000 lances pendant 5 mois. C'est évidemment invraisemblable; une telle somme représentait la quasi totalité de l'obligation de Grégoire XI envers Amédée VI." This is precisely why the sum seems to me so probable.

coin broke up the high command of the Church in Romagna. Cardinal Pierre d'Estaing, who had been in the field and absent from Bologna in the spring of 1373, although still unquestionably in charge just after Montechiari,[72] soon asked for relief from his heavy responsibilities. In the summer a new vicar general was appointed, Guillaume Noellet, the cardinal of S. Angelo. D'Estaing was then promoted cardinal bishop of Ostia, but this may have been a screen for the pope's displeasure. D'Estaing's departure was certainly marked with something like disgrace, for the Bolognese were forbidden to waste the resources of their lord the pope on expensive farewell demonstrations and gifts.[73] Hugues de la Roche was out as captain of the northern Church army, but as the pope's sister's husband he continued as marshal of the Curia.

After a Consistory in which the votes for continued war were in the majority, Gregory XI was eager as ever to crush the Visconti. He met with his chamberlain and treasurer, his Italian secretary Niccolò d'Osimo, and Giovanni Albergotti, the bishop of Arezzo, only to discuss the financial means of doing so.[74] A letter from Bernabò of 13 January prompted an angry reply on 2 February; the pope was still grimly certain that he was in the situation of a merchant accosted by a robber: either the Visconti or the clergy would have to perish.[75]

In March 1374, as a third wave of plague began both in Italy and around Avignon, the concerted action of the league was delayed while another captain, the Gascon condottiere Bernard de la Salle, was approached with an offer to take command of its army. The league as renegotiated was sealed at Villeneuve-lès-Avignon on 30 April 1374, and the far-sighted Bernabò, perhaps imagining the effect of Bernard's Gascons — and possibly Breton brigades as well — on the harvest, the forests, and the hunting of his country, begged for peace, this time credibly. On 17 July the pope secretly gave his chamberlain full powers to negotiate a truce with the Visconti, and hostilities practically ended.[76]

---

[72] In March Galeazzo Malatesta came to reside in Bologna in d'Estaing's absence: Theiner 2, no. 551. EFR *Grégoire XI secrètes France*, no. 2957 (22 May 1373): the pope rejoiced over the victory, ordered the soldiers of the Church army to join Amadeo by the safest route, and promised that their overdue stipends would be paid. It seems possible that the cardinal received the letter in Avignon and carried it back to Italy.

[73] Theiner 2, no. 555.

[74] Segrè, ed., "I dispacci," 66: Dispatch XI, dated 14 December, belongs to 1373 not 1374.

[75] *Annales ecclesiastici* 26:239–40; Segrè, ed., "I dispacci," 69, but note that dispatch XII, dated 11 February, belongs to 1374 not 1375.

[76] The league treaty is edited in EFR *Grégoire XI secrètes autres*, no. 2627. EFR *Grégoire XI secrètes France* no. 3461 notes de Cros' warrant to negotiate the Visconti truce, which is edited in Calendar Appendix A2 on the enclosed compact disk. Theiner 2, no. 562 is the pope's warrant to Giovanni Albergotti, bishop of Arezzo, and Amadeo of Savoy to make a truce with Galeazzo Visconti, 30 July 1374. Early in 1375 Cardinal

The political cost of the heavy subsidies raised in the Patrimony for the war in Lombardy then came due for payment. Florence was frightened by the aggressive potential of the new war fund if it should go to Hawkwood, and the hard-squeezed payers of the subsidy, the papal cities, were ripe for secession when Florence unfurled the banner of Liberty in 1375.[77]

In January 1375 the pope was compelled to answer certain protests of Florence against du Puy's tyrannical proceedings. When the war subsidy was blamed for discontent in the Papal States later that year, the pope disowned the subsidy as excessive, and in September he determined to recall du Puy and replace him with a cardinal legate, Pierre Flandrin.[78] Bernard de la Salle, still under contract to the Camera, set off in October by sea for Corneto with 200 men-at-arms to stiffen the garrison of the rebellious Perugia.[79] He was able, at great cost, to hold just the beachhead castle of Corneto for the pope. In November, before Flandrin could take up the legate's post, Città di Castello rebelled, followed immediately by Perugia and most of the other papal cities. Francesco di Vico, hereditary prefect of Rome and veteran rebel against papal sovereignty, liberated Viterbo and Montefiascone into his own lordship. Du Puy's severity now appeared to the pope in a different light, and he was among nine new cardinals created on 20 December.[80] The pope transferred his rage from the Visconti to the Florentines, and while he held firm to his plan to go to Italy, he now realized that circumstances might dictate where he could safely land and whether he could go to Rome.[81]

Pierre de Cros opened hostilities against the Florentine commercial nation in Avignon by summoning it to an assembly and demanding a tallage of 30,000 francs to be paid within three days. A select delegation complained of his harshness to the pope, who declared that he himself had imposed the tallage, because Florence was waging war against him in Italy with the profits of their usuries in Avignon, that he was gathering allies and opening a judicial process aimed at excommunication and interdict, and that he was willing to get his feet wet,

---

Guillaume Noellet received a similar warrant: Theiner 2, no. 575. Noellet's truce, 4 June 1375, is edited in *Codex Italiae diplomaticus*, 3:255 ff.

[77] The causes were cogently demonstrated by Glénisson, "Les origines de la révolte de l'Etat pontifical en 1375."

[78] Segrè, ed., "I dispacci," 79 and 81.

[79] Calendar no. 588.

[80] Theiner 2, nos. 567, 591.

[81] Segrè, ed., "I dispacci," 82–83: dispatch of 31 December 1375. For the Prefect di Vico and Viterbo, see Cesare Pinzi, *Storia della città di Viterbo* (Viterbo, 1899), 1:368–93; and Feliciano Bussi, *Istoria della città di Viterbo* (Rome, 1742), 208–11. Supplies to Francesco and Battista di Vico and their supporters were embargoed shortly after the Interdict on Florence: EFR *Grégoire XI secrètes autres*, nos. 3931, 3932.

presumably in their blood. They departed shaken, and they paid 20,000 francs the next day.[82]

In January 1376 the pope asked reinforcements for Bologna from Francesco Carrara, imperial vicar in Padua, but in vain: Bologna expelled its papal legate on 20 March and joined the League of Liberty.[83] Then the judicial process at Avignon against the Florentines, charging them with crimes against the clergy in Florence and with fostering sedition in the papal cities with money and rhetoric, came to a sentence: Gregory outlawed them and interdicted their city on 31 March 1376.[84] The Florentines of Avignon were stripped of their properties and driven out like dogs.[85] The pope asked Niccolò Spinelli, the queen's seneschal of Provence, to imprison the agents of Florentine merchant banks at Nice and Marseille.[86]

Most seriously, he sent Cardinal Robert of Geneva as legate *a latere* with an army to take strong measures against the rebel cities, first concluding the peace with Milan.[87] The legate enrolled in the service of the Church the Breton companies of Jean de Malestroit and Silvestre Budes, who had been menacing Avignon but who now expressed their willingness to fight in Italy.[88] The cardinal paraded the Breton companies at Carpentras in May 1376 and contracted for two months' service at 31,000 florins. Later in the summer, possibly after some tactical training, he renegotiated and settled for six months at 18 florins per month per effective lance, and they marched off to spread terror in the pope's name in Italy. When he had brought it into Emilia, he joined this army of some 10,000 troops with the company of John Hawkwood against Bologna. Early in July the cardinal occupied Modena and began to invest Bologna, where Roberto da Camerino was in command as general of the League of Liberty. The cardinal ordered a massacre at Montegiorgio to terrorize Bologna. The long-negotiated peace with Milan was finally sealed in the cardinal's camp on 9 July. Ordered south to secure central Italy for the pope's return, he lifted his siege of Bologna

---

[82] Segrè, ed., "I dispacci," 84–85.

[83] Theiner 2, no. 566.

[84] The futile defense of the Florentine attorneys, the sentence of Interdict, and a bull granting certain exemptions from the sentence were edited for the first time in full in Daniel Williman and Karen Corsano, "The Interdict of Florence (31 March 1376): New Documents," *Rivista di Storia della Chiesa in Italia* 56 (2002): 421–81, here 463–77.

[85] Segrè, ed., "I dispacci," 87: dispatch of 15 May 1376; the treasurer in October appointed a deputy procurator fiscal to gather the properties of the Florentines "qui solebant habitare in Comitatu Venaysini et civitate Avinionis ac eorum districtu": Calendar no. 617.

[86] Theiner 2:594.

[87] Baluze-Mollat 1:422–25.

[88] Segrè, ed., "I dispacci," 85–86; a good summary of the cardinal's activity is Marc Dykmans, "Clemente VII, antipapa," *Dizionario biografico degli Italiani* 26 (Rome, 1982), 222–37.

and entered the Romagna. The Breton and English troops foraged and plundered from their winter billets at Cesena, Forlì, Faenza, and Rimini.

D. Return of the Curia to Italy

There were hints from the very beginning of his pontificate that Gregory XI would return the Curia to Italy. When the time came to do so, the Treasury was nearly empty and the pope had to press his fellow monarchs for loans. Early in 1374 Louis duke of Anjou had made it possible for the pope to plan for his departure by promising to lend him the necessary money when the time came. The treasurer of Charles V of France delivered 60,000 francs to Avignon on 19 August 1376, and the next month Charles II of Navarre gave 30,000 florins of Aragon. The duke of Anjou sent 60,000 francs from Carcassonne to Avignon on 16 September 1376, and on the 20th the treasurer delivered it at Marseille in the traveling chest of 88,713 florins.[89] This loan was originally not to be secured by any pawn of treasure, only by the pope's promise to repay; and Gregory had taken the duke's testament under apostolic protection, in effect guaranteeing repayment of the loan to the duke's heirs even if both parties should die.[90] But when the cash was actually paid over, the pope had to pledge "our goods and those of the Church and the Camera present and future" for repayment. This first loan was to be paid in thirds in the course of 1377. Meanwhile, on 24 June 1377 the duke lent to the treasurer at Avignon a further 40,000 francs, repayable in halves at Midsummer and Christmas 1377.[91] None of the terms could be met. The whole debt was prorogued to Easter 1378, but by then Gregory XI was dead. His first successor Urban VI ignored the debt, but Clement VII of Avignon later satisfied it by providing galleys for the Italian expedition of Louis of Anjou.[92]

---

[89] Louis of Anjou's major affairs are chronicled by Claude Devic and Joseph Vaissete, *Histoire générale de Languedoc* (Toulouse, 1885), 9:821–69, chaps. 62–92. For the documents related to the loans, see Mirot, "Les rapports," 113–44. Gregory's efforts with the emperor Charles IV, Charles V of France, Charles II of Navarre, and Louis of Anjou have been tracked by Stefan Weiss, "Kredite europäischer Fürsten für Gregor XI.: Zur Finanzierung der Rückkehr des Papsttums von Avignon nach Rom," *Quellen und Forschungen aus italienischen Archiven und Bibliotheken* 77 (1997): 176–205. Weiss disputes the received opinion that the French court opposed the return of the pope to Rome.

[90] The bull *Eximie devotionis sinceritas*, 1 January 1374, originals cited in Bernard Barbiche, *Les actes pontificaux originaux des Archives nationales de Paris*, 3: *1305–1415* (Vatican City, 1982), 345, nos. 3083 and 3084.

[91] Mirot, "Les rapports," 116–19. See Calendar Appendix A5 on the enclosed compact disk for the text of the pope's letters of 1376 and 1377 promising repayment of 100,000 florins total.

[92] For the long-term costs of the loan, Jean Favier, "Les galées de Louis d'Anjou," in *Horizons marins, itinéraires spirituels (Ve-XVIIIe siècles)*, ed. Henri Dubois et al. (Paris,

In mid-1374 the projected date for the Curia's departure was September 1375. Venice and Pisa offered galleys for that date, and the duke of Austria promised an armed escort in case the pope should travel by land. In March 1375 the Cameral clerk Bertrand Raffin was dispatched to prepare the Vatican palace for use and to assess and seal the cardinals' *libratae* at Rome, Viterbo, and Montefiascone: in short, to serve as *taxator domorum*.[93] But in August 1375, hoping for some success in the peace conference at Bruges, the pope put the journey off until immediately after the next Easter (13 April 1376); in November, the target was 1 May 1376.[94] Cardinal Tebaldeschi sailed on 11 July 1376, expecting to greet the pope at Ostia on 20 September.[95]

As the time approached for the transfer of the Curia, Pierre de Cros pressed the clerks of the Camera to bring their records up to date. Cristoforo Tolomei remarked that registration in the Camera was nearly complete in November 1375, and in Collectoriae 356 we see the truth of the observation. The volume even includes a list of the collectories and their collectors, accurate for that month and subsequently emended.[96] At about the same time the pope's Italian and French secretaries Niccolò d'Osimo and Nicolas le Diseur collected a volume of exemplary letters of Innocent VI, Urban V, and Gregory XI. Carried to Rome and then to Anagni, this model book returned to France with le Diseur; BNF, MSS. lat. 4128 and 4127 are copies, made in the seventeenth century before the original was lost. Tolomei also noticed a number of mattresses being made, probably for packing. The chamberlain had charge of the papal *triregnum* and other regalia, and he visited the Treasury early in August 1376 with the pope's confessor Pierre Ameilh de Brénac as his witness, to take five mitres, a pontifical ring (a garnet surrounded with pearls), and a pair of gloves embroidered with silver.[97]

From mid-September 1376 to mid-January 1377 the pope and chamberlain were making their painful way by a stormy sea to Rome, almost entirely out of touch with events on shore. The *Itinerarium Gregorii XI*, a first-hand account of the journey by Pierre Ameilh de Brénac, bishop of Sinigaglia, the pope's confessor and librarian, has few admirers because of its unskillful Latin and poor verse. But the historian of the papal court and of Pierre de Cros must be attentive and grateful to Ameilh for his careful notation of dates, places, and persons, even though he sometimes shrouds the data in fustian. An Appendix at the end of this

---

1987), 2, *Marins, navires et affaires*, 137–46.

[93] Theiner 2, nos. 564, 570–73, 577; Calendar no. 433. When Gregory finally landed at Corneto, however, Viterbo was occupied by the Prefect di Vico and Montefiascone was also in rebellion.

[94] Segrè, ed., "I dispacci," 76, 79, 81.

[95] Segrè, ed., "I dispacci," 92: dispatch of 17 July 1376.

[96] Segrè, ed., "I dispacci," 81; Calendar no. 600.

[97] Hoberg, *Inventare*, 541.

book provides an English summary of the *Itinerarium*.[98] The journey of about 160 kilometers or 100 miles by river and road to Marseille took ten days. Seasonal storms caused long delays, and the sea voyage of perhaps 800 kilometers or 475 miles lasted three and a half months. In contrast, Urban V had required little more than the month of May 1367 to travel from Avignon to Corneto.[99]

The pope and his household left Avignon on Saturday 13 September. The chamberlain entertained them in his own archiepiscopal summer palace at Salon on their roundabout route to Marseille.[100] The pope stayed twelve days at S. Victor de Marseille, then boarded the galley of Ancona. Terrified by storms, some couriers vowed to go home if they survived, and de Cros granted them leave from Villefranche (Calendar no. 618). Political negotiations detained the pope at Genoa from 18 to 28 October. In storms and high winds through November some galleys were lost and the fleet separated, the chamberlain and several officials finding shelter at Port'Ercole, the pope at Elba. They were reunited at Piombino, where the pope dated an unusual letter under his wax seal to the syndics and Council of Avignon on 25 November.[101] On 5 December the fleet reached Corneto (modern Tarquinia), where the people ended their rebellion, loudly welcoming the pope and denouncing the Prefect di Vico. Here, on 21 December, the People of Rome agreed to acclaim Gregory XI as lord of the city when he entered.[102] After forty days' rest, on 13 January 1377 the pope sailed, arriving at Ostia the next day. Then there were four weary, glorious days of progress through cheering Roman crowds, and finally the pope slept in the Vatican Palace.

Each of the major conflicting interests in Italy shifted at the beginning of 1377 when the pope arrived in triumph in Rome. Francesco di Vico found his Florentine connection an embarrassment: he immediately reneged on his contribution to the League effort in the Patrimony. At the end of the year the Prefect was reconciled yet again to the pope, who baptized a daughter of his, brought from Viterbo for the purpose, with the name Gregoria.[103]

---

[98] Pierre Ronzy, *Le voyage de Grégoire XI ramenant la papauté d'Avignon à Rome (1376–1377) suivi du texte latin et de la traduction française de l'*Itinerarium Gregorii XI *de Pierre Ameilh* (Florence, 1952). This is the most accessible edition, but Ronzy's understanding of the Curia and of the topography is sometimes imperfect.

[99] The two voyages are described in parallel by Pierrette and Robert Merceron, "Retour de la papauté à Rome," *Lemouzi* 57 (1977): 40–50; and see the analytical summary by Léon Mirot, *La politique pontificale et le retour du Saint-Siège à Rome en 1376* (Paris, 1899), 156–69.

[100] Here the "Tour de Pierre de Cros" dominates the Château de l'Empéri, now the home of a military museum and a folk museum.

[101] Edited in Calendar Appendix A4 on the enclosed compact disk.

[102] Theiner 2:590–91, no. 606.

[103] Baluze-Mollat 1:427–29; Bussi, *Istoria di Viterbo*, 211; Theiner 2, no. 625.

Early in February 1377 the Breton mercenary companies, under the orders of the Cardinal of Geneva and with the help of Hawkwood's English, sacked Cesena and massacred perhaps four thousand of its people. As warfare, the terror served the Church's cause well: it broke up the Florentine League. Bologna got a truce on 17 March, and made its submission and was reconciled before the pope sitting in judgement at Anagni on 4 July (Calendar no. 625). The chamberlain was in attendance, and just a year later he was to preside at the same tribunal to determine that Urban VI's election had been null and void.

Florence remained stubbornly unrepentant, and Gregory XI continued the interdict. On Ascension Thursday, 7 May, the pope "sat in judgement as on Holy Thursday" to intensify the anathemas.[104] The queen of Naples approved, the pope imposed, and the chamberlain exacted a subsidy in the south to continue the war.[105] The unpredictable Breton troops, although they frightened the Curia, worried Florence more, enough to force the peace agreement of Sarzana in March 1378, just before the death of Gregory XI. Urban VI finally ratified the peace at Tivoli on 26 July.

The pope left the Vatican for his summer retreat on 16 May 1377, first paying two weeks of visits to the major churches of Rome, S. John Lateran and S. Mary Major, arriving in Anagni on 2 June. He was away from Rome more than five months, staying at Anagni with a small household, but with eighteen cardinals, and returning to Rome on 7 November.[106]

The duke of Anjou was dunning the pope for the repayment of his loan, reminding him of the 120 notable fortresses which he had recovered from the English. Gregory replied with a flattering letter asking delay of payment,[107] but the duke did not immediately relent. Early in 1378, in a long letter, close and partially in cipher, the pope prodded his treasurer at Avignon to press the collectors for the cash to pay the overdue debt, forestalling as long as possible the sale of items from the treasure.[108]

---

[104] Franz Ehrle, "Die Chronik des Garoscus de Ulmoisca Veteri und Bertrand Boysset," *Archiv für Literatur- und Kulturgeschichte des Mittelalters* 7 (1900): 311–420, here 329.

[105] Lunt, *Papal Revenue*, 2:216: a quittance (10 June 1377) by Johannes, abbot of S. Giovanni in Venere, collector in Abruzzi, for payment on a subsidy, recently imposed by Gregory XI, for the emergency caused by the wicked Florentines; the assessments were contained in the collector's commission by Pierre de Cros. The pope added his own letter to those of Pierre de Cros and cardinals Jean de la Grange and Pierre Flandin, asking Silvester Budes to take his orders from Cardinal Pierre d'Estaing: *Grégoire XI secrètes France*, no. 2038, ed. from BNF, MS. lat. 4127.

[106] Ehrle, "Die Chronik des Bertrand Boysset," 330.

[107] 12 October 1377, cited by Devic and Vaissete, *Histoire générale de Languedoc*, 9:862 from a manuscript in the collection of C. J. Colbert, bishop of Montpellier.

[108] Edited in Calendar Appendix A6 on the enclosed compact disk.

The minimal papal court in the last eight months of Gregory XI presents an odd and melancholy scene. The pope was ill and distracted, bypassing his chamberlain and trying to manage the finances of the Church with personal letters to his treasurer more than a month's travel away in Avignon. For his secret political correspondence he was relying on two private secretaries. These were Niccolò d'Osimo, who died at Anagni before November 1377, and Nicolas le Diseur, whose confidential service the pope shared — perhaps more than he knew — with Charles V of France.[109] The king richly rewarded "nostre amé et feal maistre Nicole le Diseur, secretaire de nostre saint père le pape et le nostre," ordering a grand purse of 40 francs paid to him at the end of 1377 for drafting bulls in the king's favor against the bishop of Saintes over the lordship of La Rochelle.[110] The two secretaries certainly kept their own registers of the letters which they drafted. Niccolò's register is lost, but le Diseur's went to France and survives in copies.[111] Apart from this, we have no registers of secret and curial letters from the last eighteen months of Gregory XI. The chancery did not operate at all during the four-month voyage, and only common letters were registered at Rome by the staff under the deputy vice-chancellor, Archbishop Bartolomeo Prignano.[112] The pope had had enough of the sinecure in Avignon of Pierre de Monteruc the cardinal vice-chancellor, and he offered the post to the king of France to confer, if Pierre de Monteruc should fail to come to the Curia by Pentecost 1378.[113]

Wherever the chamberlain may have spent the months when we have no notice of him in Anagni, he did have a house in the Vatican palace, frescoed and decked with his arms, its street windows protected with iron wickets.[114] He held the treasure in safekeeping in the Castel S. Angelo, and it was probably at his inspiration that the dying pope made the castellan swear not to surrender the

---

[109] Gane, *Chapitre de Notre-Dame*, 343, no. 383.

[110] Léopold Delisle, ed., *Mandements et actes divers de Charles V (1364–1380)* (Paris, 1874), 776, no. 1555. I have not found these letters in the editions of originals or registers of Gregory XI, but the legal question was one on which the pope had offered justice in a letter of 30 October 1373: EFR *Grégoire XI secrètes France*, no. 1432.

[111] EFR *Grégoire XI secrètes France*, nos. 2031–2119, with an introduction, cols. 677–680.

[112] Ottenthal, *Regulae*, 43, rule no. 86 (1 February 1377) allows for beneficial letters to be dated 13 September 1376 if they were requested earlier; rules nos. 91 and 92 refer to letters of justice.

[113] Rey-Courtel, "Les cardinaux du Midi," 53–54.

[114] By an instrument drawn by Guillelmus de Alberia on 17 March 1377, Bertrand du Mazel paid 13 current florins to "Jacobus Jaqueti de regione Capitolii et Petrus Alexi de regione Transtiberis pro pictura per eos facta in hospitio d. camerarii et pro remutatione scutorum ubi sunt arma domini nostri et sua per ipsos in dicto hospitio factorum"; witnesses Jean de Beauvais (Mende) and Guillaume Vidal (Toulouse); on 3 April Mazel paid £19.17.6 to "Guillelmo Yvonis fabro pro 2 gossetis sive campsogueriis": RA 200, 641v, ed. Kirsch, *Rückkehr* and (less accurately) Mirot, *Politique*, 175 n.

fortress to anyone without the written consent of the cardinals at Avignon.[115] De Cros also attempted to control the impending conclave. The electoral statute *Futuris periculis*, attributed to Gregory XI a week before his death, may well have been the creation of Pierre de Cros, and it is impossible to know how fully or how consciously it was authorized by the pope himself. No original exists, and the letter is known only from an awkwardly registered version, labeled "de Camera," which Marc Dykmans has analyzed with the gravest suspicion: he gives good reasons to consider it a simple forgery.[116]

After the death of Gregory XI and the coronation of Urban VI, it was rumored that another undispatched letter had been found in the late pope's private chest, a letter by which he ordered the treasurer at Avignon to pay the ransom of Roger de Beaufort, 400,000 francs.[117] The story has the ring of general truth, but the sum was unconscionable and impossible and the letter was neither sent nor registered, whoever may have written it. True or not, the story is a wry summary of the political economy of Gregory XI's last months, indeed of his whole pontificate, trapped in the wars of France and Italy. Pierre de Cros refused to recognize the election of Bartolomeo Prignano and labored to overturn it. By the end of October he was chamberlain to a new pope, Clement VII of Avignon, and the Western Schism had begun.[118]

---

[115] Gandelin's uncle Pierre Rostaing, who shared the command of the Castel, told of the oath in a letter to the king of Castile, edited from BNF, MS. lat. 11745, fol. 64v in Baluze-Mollat 2:729. Urban VI wrote to the cardinals at Avignon on 15 June 1378, calling the story false but nevertheless asking them to write the required release: the original letter close is IM 2991.

[116] "La bulle de Grégoire XI à la veille du Grand Schisme," *Mélanges* 89 (1977): 485–95.

[117] Segrè, ed., "I dispacci," 271.

[118] Howard Kaminsky, "The Great Schism," in *The New Cambridge Medieval History*, 6: *c. 1300 - c. 1415* (Cambridge, 2000), 674–96, here 674–78; Williman, "Schism within the Curia."

4. The Sources and the Calendar

A. Diplomatic Sketch

The official correspondence of Pierre de Cros' predecessors, the chamberlains Etienne Cambarou and Arnaud Aubert, were routinely registered. The history of the practice is explained in my calendars of their letters, and need not be repeated.[1] Most of the letters in the present Calendar are known from registered copies or registered notes, but there are a few original letters and instruments as well.

Most of the items in this Calendar are formal letters patent. The texts of such letters began with the chamberlain's name and titles in the nominative, the name of those addressed in the dative, and the greeting itself, usually "salutem" in the accusative. They are called letters patent or open because their seal, the almond-shaped great seal in this case, did not close the letter; instead it hung by a parchment tape from the folded bottom edge of the letter. A letter patent of the chamberlain was usually composed by himself or by one of the clerks of the Camera, if the matter or the circumstances were novel and a new text had to be created. Otherwise one of the notaries could be given the raw data — the persons' names, the type of business, the sums and terms — and could be trusted to adapt a model letter from the earlier registers or from his own collection of exemplars. The rhetorical style of these letters was rather graceless, ponderous officialese, varied with sophomoric flourishes which sometimes fail grammatically.[2]

The notary would write out or "engross" the letter on a parchment sheet, fold up the bottom edge and add the name of a clerk, if one of these was responsible, on the fold. The notary would then cut a slit through the two layers of parchment, pass a parchment tape through the slits, write his own initials on the tape, and then affix the chamberlain's great seal in wax (normally red) backed by a paper wafer. If a fee was demanded for the letter, the sum was written under the

---

[1] D. Williman, "Letters of Etienne Cambarou, Camerarius Apostolicus (1347–1361)," *Archivum Historiae Pontificiae* 15 (1977): 195–215; and idem, *Calendar of the Letters of Arnaud Aubert, Camerarius Apostolicus (1361–1371)* (Toronto, 1992), 50–53.

[2] Evidence for this severe judgement from Calendar no. 80 is deposed in my tribute to my colleague Saul Levin: D. Williman, "A Sad Moment for Official Rhetoric," *General Linguistics* 35 (1995): 177–80.

fold.[3] More solemn documents, such as the letters publishing the imperial bulls against the Visconti in 1374, were sealed on cords and the seals cupped in undyed beeswax. The same great seal was used on notarial instruments which recorded acts of the chamberlain.

When a letter was close, it was written with less rhetorical formality and began with an address in the vocative. A letter close was folded up, pierced, and sealed in such a way that the seal tape would have to be cut before the letter could be read: the seal guaranteed the secrecy of the letter. The names of the sender and receiver had to be written on the outside of the sealed letter. The seal used for letters close was normally the signet, mounted on the chamberlain's ring.

The same notary who engrossed a letter or instrument would usually register it as well, copying either the full text or an abridged note of the essential data in a parchment-covered paper volume prepared in advance, the current office register. Sometimes the registry preceded and sometimes it followed the engrossing of the letter.[4]

B. The Seal and Signet of Pierre de Cros

The great seal *camerariatus officii* of Pierre de Cros exists in a few examples, attached to letters patent, and three of those which I have seen remain in sufficiently good condition to reveal the seal's meaningful features.[5]

---

[3] L. M. Bååth, *Diplomatarium Svecanum, Acta Cameralia* (Stockholm, 1942), 2, *1371–1492*, no. 805 is an original parchment letter patent of Pierre de Cros in the Riksarkivet, Stockholm, dated 23 June 1372. "Adest sigillum, sed detritum. In taenia sigilli pergamenea: R. Sub plica: V flor. V gr. In plica a sinistra manu propria: P. de Albiartis. A dextra: Receptum est. A tergo alia manu: Quitantia de CCLXX florenis, item de LV florenis." This is a quittance to Berengarius, archbishop of Upsala, for 270 fl. common services and 53 fl. minute services; the letter was registered in OS 39, 269^v.

[4] Administrative letters of the chamberlain Pierre de Cros are listed by R. H. Bautier and J. Sornay, *Les sources de l'histoire économique et sociale du moyen âge*, 1: *Provence – Comtat Venaissin*, 3 vols. (Paris, 1968–1974), 1:79–80 in a table which is not perfectly accurate, and which follows the inaccurate presumption that these registers were "notarial," i.e., that each register records the instruments of a single cameral notary. Only Collectoriae 357, the personal register of Jean Rousset, was of the notarial type.

[5] The seals attached to A.A.Arm.C, 509 and 510 and to IM 2735. The seal is described in P. Sella and M.-H. Laurent, *I sigilli dell'Archivio segreto vaticano*, 3 vols. (Vatican City, 1937–1964), 1:201–5, no. 692: "Architettura gotica: in alto la Madonna a mezzo busto con il Bambino; in mezzo S. Pietro e S. Paolo; in basso un vescovo mitrato, orante, con ai lati uno scudo con le chiavi in decusse, dall'altro uno scudo: capo non ben distinto, campo tre fasce merlate. Sigillo di ceralacca rossa su supporto di cera vergine, ovale, mm. 60 x 40, appeso a cappio con un cordone di seta bianca, mancante in margine."

The Sources and the Calendar 75

FIGURE 4.1
Great Seal and Signet of Pierre de Cros
Drawings by Karen Corsano.

It is one-sided, almond- or boat-shaped, about 63 mm. from point to point and 40 mm. side to side. A full-length S. Peter with two keys (viewer's left) and S. Paul with book and sword (right), each with his halo, stand on an architrave in the central range of a Gothic shrine, below a bust of the Virgin with Child. In the lower range the archbishop chamberlain, wearing mitre and pallium, holds a processional cross in his right hand and a money-sack in his left. In its essential features this is the official portrait of a chamberlain as painted by Andrea da Firenze in the Spanish Chapel of S. Maria Novella, Florence, in 1368.[6] On the seal, the chamberlain is flanked by two shields, on the viewer's left the crossed keys of the Apostolic See and on the right the crenellated arms of de Cros. The abbreviated legend reads (downward on the right) S[IGILLVM] PETRI DOMINI (and upward on the left) PAPE CAMERARII.

The only example of the signet which I have seen is in red wax, attached to a hasty order for a month's pay to the guard of Pont-de-Sorgues dated 23 August 1380.[7] The field is nearly square, 12 mm. broad and 11 mm. high, with beveled corners. The apostles are shown from the waist up, on the left S. Peter with keys and on the right S. Paul with sword, flanking an almond shape to suggest the

---

[6] Aubert Calendar, facing p. 40.
[7] IM 3048.

chamberlain's great seal beneath the papal crossed keys. An inscription arches over all, illegible but probably an abbreviated SIGNETVM PETRI CAMERARII.

C. Sources in the Vatican Archives

Almost all the sources of letters and instruments in this Calendar are found in the Vatican Archives and listed here in alphabetical order of their *fondi*. The volumes of registers are described in some detail here; a more complete physical description of the single instruments can be found in the Calendar.

Archivum Arcis, Armarium C, no. 52: 12 January 1373. Original parchment letter close, 472 x 495 mm., seal missing. Quittance to Bertrand du Mazel (Calendar no. 260).

Archivum Arcis, Armarium C, nos. 509 and 510: 11 October 1372. The chamberlain's vidimus of two imperial bulls against Bernabò Visconti (Calendar nos. 185, 186).

Collectoriae 51, 345r-368v: early 1373. A Cameral case concerning the shipment of provisions from Burgundy to Cardinal Francesco Tebaldeschi, including some letters of the chamberlain (Calendar nos. 391, 392, 400, 401).

Collectoriae 257 is the paper account book of Guido de Ruppe for Tours, 1366-1372 (Calendar no. 194).

Collectoriae 356: "Regestum Litterarum Camerarii Apostolici 1375." A large volume, 28 x 37 cm. Paper, watermark a bow and (82 mm.) arrow. 98 folia, bound and numbered before the writing of the register; 89 folia written, plus an original parchment half-cover, now numbered fol. 97, with a late Cameral note verso: "Jacominus Josef de civitate Virdunensi, habitator Avinionis, fuit receptus in cursorem die 2 Martii anno '85." The original roman-numeral foliation is written in the upper right corner (lost to rot in fols. 1–17), and the automatic stamped numeration in the lower right; but fol. xix is missing. 1r: "Ave Maria. Sequela registri litterarum d. Camerarii domini nostri pape concessarum sub annis et diebus ac tenoribus infrascriptis." 1r-67v is a register from 16 December 1374 to 9 January 1376. 44v blank; 5 blank folia 68–72, the end of a quire; 6 blank folia 73–78. 79r-82v contain 2 later complete letters, 26 April and 14 May 1376, and one (tailless because a page is missing), 7 May 1376. 83rv blank, the beginning of a new quire. 84r-89v a spaciously written list of collectors. This volume was probably written with a view to the transfer to Italy: in his dispatch of 22 November 1375 Cristoforo Tolomei said that he could see in the palace no sign of a coming departure "nisi quod libri et jura Camere registrantur in magna frequentia et quaxi registrati sunt."[8] One subscription of a Cameral notary appears on 22v: "de

---

[8] Segrè, ed., "I dispacci," 81.

Solegiis." This volume contains two references, on 53v and 178r (Calendar nos. 135 and 146), to a register of 1374, a volume of at least 141 folia which is regrettably not known to survive.

Collectoriae 357 was a blank book, watermark a S. John's eagle, used mostly as a notarial register by Jean Rousset. The first 16 folia, left blank at first for a table of contents, were eventually used to copy the will (26 August 1381) of Card. Simon de Brossano 6r-7v. 18 letters and instruments from the time of chamberlain Arnaud Aubert (1368–1370) loosely occupy 17r-34r. The register was picked up again under Pierre de Cros: on 47r-67v, 11 instruments (18 July 1371–28 April 1372); on 70r-74r, 4 instruments (March 1381 - March 1383).

Collectoriae 358: "Regestum litterarum camerarii apostolici Gregorii XI 1371–1373 et Clementis VII 1378–1387." The volume was bound in advance: uniform gatherings, mostly octernions, all watermarked a cheese or weight 92 mm. high. The numeration of folios is by automatic stamp, lower right recto. This register did not travel to Italy. It was written in seven stages:

I. 1r, a short parchment sheet remaining of the cover, with the title "Domini Gregorii pape XImi. Regestum novum diversarum commissionum inceptum die nono Julii anno LXXprimo que transierant sub sigillo domini camerarii archiepiscopi Arelatensis" in cursive, then repeated in a larger, clearer Gothic display hand.

2r-7v were left blank for a table of contents which was never supplied; later a letter of 14 September 1372 was registered on 3r.

8r-142r a register, June 1371–January 1373. The letter which began the register was of 9 July 1371, but the earliest date in it is 28 June 1371 (9r-10r).

II. 163r-172r register of chaplains of honor, 1371.[9]

III. 179v-180v, 186v-187v, 193v and back cover 194rv: a register of the dispatch of papal and Cameral letters.

IV. 143r-148v vidimus of two imperial bulls (October 1372), registry suspended; 159v-160v, 176v-177r, 188r afterthoughts of 1372.

V. 142v, 177v, 189v: afterthoughts of 1375–1377.

VI. 149r-158v, 173r-176v, 178rv, 181rv, 190v, 192v: register of Pierre de Cros, 20 June 1380–12 November 1383.

VII. 191v-192r a letter of François de Conzié, 1387.

Collectoriae 359A, 16v-18r. Memoranda of papal decisions for the Camera, in part a copy of RA 198, 504r-508v, edited in Samaran-Mollat 234–35. Samaran accounts for this dossier:[10] "Les autres documents qui dans le volume 359A (Coll.) accompagnent la copie des instructions d'Urbain V méritent aussi

---

[9] Cited by Oscar von Mitis, "Curiale Eidregister: Zwei Amtsbücher aus der Kammer Martins V.," *Mitteilungen des Instituts für österreichische Geschichtsforschung*, Ergänzungsband 6 (Innsbruck, 1901), 413–48, here 420.

[10] "La jurisprudence pontificale en matière de droit de dépouilles (*jus spolii*) dans le second moitié du XIVe siècle," *Mélanges* 2 (1902): 141-56, here 146 n.

une attention spéciale. Il semble que dans ce cahier, relié par erreur avec un registre de lettres camérales de Clément VII, le pape Grégoire XI ou son camérier aient voulu réunir comme dans une sorte de mémorandum les actes financiers les plus importants promulgués par les papes du XIVe siècle. On y trouve des bulles de Jean XXII, de Clément VI, d'Innocent VI, d'Urbain V, de Grégoire XI. L'extravagante de Boniface VIII sur les dîmes, insérée au Corpus juris canonici (Extr. comm. 3.7.1) y figure même sous la forme d'une confirmation par Innocent VI."

Collectoriae 375. A soft-bound volume of 80 paper folia in 2 great gatherings; a note on cover "Compotum d. Cardinalis Ambianensis [Johannis de Grangia] expediatur per vidimus."

1–30 accounts, from the time of John XXII and earlier.

31–80 (watermark scissors, 84 mm.) Receipts of common services and other taxes, and expenses, mostly for the payment of German mercenaries in November [1375].[11] One instrument 50r-52r noted as witnessed by Elias de Vodro, clerk of the Camera, Jacobus de Solegiis notary, and m. Johannes Benedicti de S. Angelo, notary of Urbino, and Guillelmus Secoclausa for stipend of d. Nicolaus alias dictus Nichil, miles Alamannie, at Vercelli, 20 November [1375].

Collectoriae 393, 52r-95r (8 October 1376–19 March 1379). A miscellaneous volume. Spine: "Miscellanea Cameralia 1375 1383 & Zifrae Clem. VII Collect. [faint pencil:] 381.A 393." The letters of the Camera in folia 52–84 begin with the title "Sequitur Regestrum diversarum litterarum \\a tempore quo dominus noster recessit de Avinione emanatarum, et plurimarum scripturarum tangentium Cameram Apostolicam.//" This is a register kept at Avignon of incoming and outgoing letters and instruments, October 1376–July 1379. It was maintained for the treasurer until the chamberlain returned to Avignon, in advance of the Curia, in February 1379. Folia 56v-57v, 66v, 71v-72v, 80v-81v are blank. 85r-95r is a headless fragment of a register, kept by the roving nuncio Bertrand du Mazel, of papal and chamberlain's letters, here 1 September 1377–19 March 1379.[12] Mazel's copy on 89rv (Calendar no. 638, 12 February 1378) by chance repeats the treasurer's 64v.[13]

The Instrumenta miscellanea which appear in the Calendar are mostly drafts and undispatched letters.

IM 2660: 30 August 1371 (Calendar no. 17)

IM 2661: 19 September 1371 (Calendar no. 21)

---

[11] Stephan Selzer, *Deutsche Söldner im Italien des Trecento* (Tübingen, 2001), 257, n. 430.

[12] For this energetic and necessary agent of the Camera, see Jean Glénisson, "Un agent de la Chambre apostolique au XIVe siècle: Les missions de Bertrand du Mazel (1364–1378)," *Mélanges* 59 (1947): 89–119.

[13] This is the volume cited by R. C. Trexler, *The Spiritual Power: Republican Florence under Interdict* (Leiden, 1974) as Collectiones 93.

IM 2664: 23 September 1371 (Calendar no. 22)
IM 2669: 26 October 1371 (Calendar no. 23)
IM 2672: 4 December 1371 (Calendar no. 29)
IM 2697: 30 October 1372 (Calendar no. 201)
IM 2715: 15 January 1373 (Calendar no. 262)
IM 2716: 1 February 1373 (Calendar no. 262)
IM 2729: 27 March 1373 (Calendar no. 301)
IM 2735: 29 March 1373 (Calendar no. 303)
IM 2794: 20 July 1373 (Calendar no. 326)
IM 2808: 17 September 1373 (Calendar no. 347)
IM 2833: 3 April 1374 (Calendar no. 385)
IM 2869: 7 November 1374 (Calendar no. 402)
IM 2871: 9 December 1374 (Calendar no. 404)
IM 2915: 28 September 1375 (Calendar no. 575)
IM 2940: 21 May 1376 (Calendar no. 611)
IM 2972: 4 July 1377 (Calendar no. 625)
IM 5155: 10 November 1372 (Calendar no. 218)
Registra Avenionensia 198: see Collectoriae 359A above.

Registra Avenionensia 220: The volume's spine bears the title: "Clemens VII" [written over "Greg. XI"] an. I part. XVI. tom. XVI" and the volume begins with curial letters of Clement VII, the first dated Fondi, 1 January anno primo.

Folia 213–376, 22 x 29 cm., watermarked with a crossbow, 100 mm. long. A register of chamberlain's letters, spaciously written in 11 quires, from 16 October 1372 to 16 December 1381. Handwritten folio numbers in the upper right recto, no automatic numbering. Many blank pages and folia. Letters between 8 March 1378 and 5 August 1378 were not registered here except in retrospect. 302r is headed "Annus Quintus." In a space between letters of 1376 (313v-314r) was inserted one dated Rome, 15 February 1378; similarly one dated Fondi, October 1378, was inserted at 322r before some letters of 1377: evidence that the register did travel to Italy with the court of Gregory XI. The sign-manual R appears in the margin of 326r, following the syllabus "Copia littere Johannis Rosseti." This volume may be in part the register of Rousset; many letters in it certainly were written in his interest. On 365–367 are several letters by the chamberlain's lieutenants at Fondi, early in 1379, captioned with their taxes. On 368r the dates go back to 1373. The rest of RA 220 is mostly chancery-register scraps and quires, but 517–538 is a dossier of papal letters in cameral affairs beginning with Clement VI.

Appendix I:
The *Itinerarium* of Pierre Ameilh[1]

Avignon to Corneto

The pope with his household departed Avignon on 13 September 1376 by barge down the Rhône, then up the Durance to Noves (27), then by road to Orgon (36). On the 16th (41) they reached Pierre de Cros' diocese of Arles, and in his palace of Salon, called the Castle of the Empire, he provided rich hospitality; the town had recently returned to obedience and he wished to display its beauties and natural riches.[2] On the 17th (53) they reached Aix and enjoyed two days' hospitality of the aged archbishop Giraud de Posilhac. On the 19th the party traveled east (65); they lunched at Trets and slept (69) at S. Maximin,[3] and the next night at Auriol, and on the 22nd (77) pressed on to Marseille in oppressive heat. The pope stayed in the ancient monastery of S. Victor and presided in a Consistory where he heard advice for and against his journey. He promoted (103) Jean de Cros, the cardinal of Limoges, cardinal bishop of Palestrina.

After 12 days' rest, (110) on 2 October, while a bitter Mistral blew, the pope boarded the galley of Ancona and (122) slept moored to the Ile Ratonneau. The 3rd brought rain and wind, but the pope's galley made Port-Miou for lunch (127) and Sanary-sur-Mer for dinner. They anchored two more stormy days on the beach "de Ronsellis,"[4] where (138) the pope's admiral Juan Fernández de Heredia took command of the flotilla. On the 6th (146) they were blown past Toulon in high seas, reaching the port of "Reneston" at sunset. At midnight (150) a horrible north wind rose, terrifying everyone to prayers and vows to S. Cyriaque. When the sea calmed the pope landed at Port-Grimaud and slept at S.

---

[1] From Ronzy, *Le voyage de Grégoire XI ramenant la papauté d'Avignon à Rome (1376-1377)*. Line numbers of the Ronzy edition appear sporadically in parentheses.

[2] Hence this overland route on muleback in preference to a galley on the Rhône. Pierre de Cros as archbishop of Arles was lord of Salon, and the "Tour de Pierre de Cros" of the Château de l'Imperi there memorializes his work of fortification.

[3] S. Maximin is far east, out of the straight line of travel to Marseille.

[4] A part of the island or group Les Ambiez.

Tropez. On the 8th they departed from "Vermigneria" with a very favorable wind and passed before the Lions off Fréjus. The abbot of S. Honorat of Lérins (Jean de Tournefort) brought gifts. The storm ended that day; they dined at Antibes, where the galleys of the cardinals of Limoges (Jean de Cros) and of Narbonne (Pierre de la Jugie) joined the pope's, and where the bishop of Grasse (Aymar de la Voute) gave so generously that Grasse was not fat any more. The 9th (170) was clear; the fleet passed by Nice and entered Villefranche and rested the day. They reached Monaco on the 10th, but then the wind, backing to northeast, blew the pope's galley back to Villefranche where it moored until the 15th. Another ship (182) was less lucky: carrying couriers, ushers, and servants, it lost its mainbrace and sails, then its anchor cable and mast. The sailors panicked; again there were prayers and vows; freight was lost and one cleric drowned, and on the 14th, the feast of S. Calixtus, they found themselves on S. Marguerite, the greater island of Lérins, 28 kilometers southwest of Villefranche.[5] The pope (201) stayed the night of the 16th onshore at Monaco, the 17th at Savona, some 36 kilometers by sea from Genoa, and (210) on Saturday the 18th he crossed the Gulf to Genoa, though there was a high sea in the evening.

Twelve days of negotiation failed to produce an alliance between the Church and the Genoese Republic. (246) The pope boarded the galley of Ancona the evening of 28 October and (258) sailed early the next day, wishing to press on to Rome, but in a day and a night his galley made only 25 kilometers against the wind and put in to Portofino at dawn of the 30th. (266) The morning of the 31st was wasted, rowing 20 miles only to be blown back to Portofino. The pope decided to walk to the monastery of S. Girolamo della Cervaia, stayed there the night, and (278) on Saturday morning, All Saints' Day, celebrated high mass and made gifts to that poor monastery.[6] (286) Catalan and Genoese sailors came to blows and the pope had to put to sea in haste without an All Souls' mass on 2 November. (298) The galleys were separated and had different luck in the high winds and seas of that day. The galley of Ancona, carrying the pope, was separated from that carrying the author Pierre Ameilh, the chamberlain, and the vice-treasurer Elie de Vodron, bishop of Catania, but both vessels weathered the storm. The galleys of Genoa, Marseille, and Aragon were damaged; one sank with the loss of two hands, while the rest were rescued by the galley of Aragon, under the command of Gilbert de Crucellis, and carried back to Portofino. (310) The 4th dawned clear and the "Red Galley" returned to Portofino, as did the galley of Ancona.

The pope stopped at Portovenere, 57 km on, that night, but seven galleys went on 70 km to Livorno, where the pope joined twelve cardinals in the castle

---

[5] Five couriers on this ship vowed to return at once to Avignon, and the chamberlain granted them leave from Villefranche: Calendar no. 618.

[6] Léon Mirot, *La politique pontificale et le retour du Saint-Siège à Rome en 1376* (Paris, 1899), 163 notes a payment of 25 fl. 5s. 6d. to the cellarer.

the next night.[7] (322) The pope arrived at Porto Pisano at the mouth of the Arno on the 6th at lunchtime, then was rowed to Livorno. Pisa and Lucca, allies of Florence, welcomed the pope and lavished gifts of food and wine on the court during its ten days' rest at Livorno. Clerics, emissaries of Florence, came to ask for the lifting of the Interdict; but they failed, not being empowered to offer the necessary submission and confession of guilt. (354) On the evening of the 14th the pope boarded another galley. The galley of Ancona departed with an advance party the next morning and, despite cloud and rain, reached Piombino, 66 km on, that night. It (362) departed before dawn the next day, Sunday the 16th, and made Port'Ercole on the far side of Orbetello after dark, a run of almost 75 km. The pope's galley (366) had been prevented by an east wind from turning in to Piombino. Then the sailors, unable to see the sun in the overcast sky, thought the northeast wind northerly and ran before it, fortunately to the island of Elba. The pope slept at Portoferraio, went by road to Porto Longone (now Porto Azzurro, on the east coast), and the next day visited the dry peak of Capoliveri. Pierre Ameilh names the pope's companions on Elba: Jean de Beaufort, archbishop of Narbonne; Pierre de Laplotte, recently abbot of Aniane, then bishop of Carpentras, papal referendarius (Jean de Bar, subdeacon, the senior cubicularius, was absent); Pierre de Chassagne, registrar of letters (whose bulls and purse were as yet safe from the sea); Elie de Vodron, bishop of Catania and treasurer;[8] Pierre Guiraudon, provost of Cavaillon; Robert Defio, papal sergeant-at-arms. (394) While the pope was on Elba a strong wind and high sea wrecked a galley of Queen Joan on Talamone; Bertrand Largier, the cardinal of Glandèves, was rescued from the sea, but he lost some members of his household and some goods. (404) The galley carrying Jean de la Grange, the cardinal of Amiens, foundered.[9] Etienne de Brandis of Marseille, admiral of the king of France, tried to ride out the storm with only one anchor to windward. Pierre Ameilh (by now an experienced and prudent sailor) knew this to be insufficient security. The anchor cable broke and the ship was caught broadside and swamped. All the people were saved, but all the cargo lost. (414) On Friday the 21st Cardinal Pierre de la Jugie, the pope's cousin, was buried in the church of Pisa. (418) At this point in

---

[7] Ronzy, *Voyage*, 88-89, note 71, provides some extra details of the pope's visit, following local chronicles. Franz Ehrle, ed., "Die Chronik des Garoscus de Ulmoisca Veteri und Bertrand Boysset," *Archiv für Literatur- und Kulturgeschichte des Mittelalters* 7 (1893-1900): 311-420 combines the chronicle's notes with background from the Camera's record of expenses on the journey (IE 345); the count of cardinals at Livorno appears on 328.

[8] Kirsch, *Rückkehr*, 195. Elias was appointed vice-treasurer to keep the ledgers during the voyage. His records are in IE 345, including Introitus to 4 January 1378 and Exitus to 24 December 1377.

[9] Kirsch, *Rückkehr*, 205-6: the pope gave Cardinal de la Grange 500 fl. to compensate him for the loss of his galley.

his narrative Pierre Ameilh thanks Pierre de Cros for his generosity, especially for having once secured him a benefice, and for the hospitality of his table at Port'Ercole. (426) Elba's resources were stretched by the pope's large company, and when the wind dropped he crossed from Portoferraio to Piombino, where the people rejoiced but gave no gifts, instead demanding money for the food which they provided.[10] (434) On Thursday the 27th the pope sailed 68 km southeast to Santa Liberata, where a causeway joins Monte Argentario to the mainland. The next day he boarded a shallow boat and crossed the northern laguna to Orbetello. He was greeted by his rector of the Patrimony, Niccolò Orsini the count of Nola, crowned with laurel, and by the expelled bishop of Montefiascone, Pierre Arsenh, in armor.[11] A bonfire was lit on Monte Argentario to announce the pope's arrival in his States. (450) The galleys of Queen Joan departed, carrying her new husband Duke Otto of Brunswick. (454) Since Orbetello's provisions were insufficient to support a long visit, the pope crossed the southern laguna and walked to Port'Ercole, boarded his galley after dark on Thursday, 4 December, and departed the next morning.

The beach (470) of Corneto (today Tarquinia) was held secure for his arrival by the papal vicar. The pope received the keys of the country. The people of Corneto, repenting their recent adherence to the rebellion of Viterbo, welcomed the pope with cries of "Long live Peace," "Lord, spare your people," and "May the Prefect die with his followers," and the pope granted his pardon.

---

[10] From Piombino the pope dispatched his letter (Calendar Appendix A4 on the enclosed compact disk) to the Council of Avignon. The chamberlain and other officials had gone ahead in the galley of Ancona, and were sheltering at Port'Ercole: Ehrle, ed., "Chronik des ... Bertrand Boysset," 327. The pope and the chamberlain exchanged letters of encouragement and news, summarized by Cristoforo Tolomei; the group at Port'Ercole also included Cardinals Orsini, d'Estaing, Corsini, and de Vergne: Segrè, ed., "I dispacci," 255; Kirsch, *Rückkehr*, 206.

[11] Ignazio Ciampi, ed., *Niccola della Tuccia, Cronaca di Viterbo* (Florence, 1872), 37 says that the fugitive treasurer Angelo Tavernini was also on the beach at Orbetello to meet the pope, but that Gregory, considering him to be criminally responsible for the rebellions in the Patrimony, ordered him to be sent away unheard, and Pierre Ameilh does not mention him.

Corneto to Rome

The Curia remained at Corneto forty days, through Christmas and the feast of Epiphany.[12] On Tuesday 13 January 1377 the pope appointed three archbishops.[13] He slept on his galley that night. Guiscard de Comborn, lord of Treignac, master-at-arms of the Household, lost his sword overboard.[14] The pope sailed safely at midnight with a calm sea and fair sky, but the lighter carrying the horses struck a rock. (29) The onshore breeze of the 14th brought the fleet to the mouth of the Tiber and after lunch the pope entered the tiny fortress city of Ostia and dined there. A party of aged Romans came to welcome the pope with torches, horns, and dancing. (37) On Friday morning the 16th he boarded the galley of Marseille which daringly raced upriver against the galley of Ancona. The pope's party landed at Porta Portese to a grand welcome of flags, belled horses, bandaresi with trumpets, and cries of "Long live our Lord." The far shore at S. Paolo fuori le mura was lined with crowds, torches, and decorations. (53) The pope spent the night on board his galley, offered two masses in the morning before landing, then was escorted to S. Paolo where he heard the mass of his confessor, the author Pierre Ameilh. He slept that night in the palace of S. Paolo and set out from there on the morning of 18 January for his procession into Rome, met by prepared pageants and the well-armed, well-drilled company of Raimond de Turenne, also the bandaresi of the city, the armed escort of the senator Gomez Albornoz, and thousands of the people in festival white. (73) Juan Fernández de Heredia carried the flag of the Church. At Porta Ostiense were all the clergy of the city, carrying papal and imperial insignia; bells and fanfares sounded as the pope crossed the threshold, and the lordship of the city was handed to him with the keys. (87) The cardinals' servants were directed to their houses by Bertrand Raffin the assignator domorum.[15] Finally at Compline the pope's party arrived, still fasting, at the Vatican Palace, where they dined by torchlight.

---

[12] According to an anonymous chronicle, Raimond de Turenne, commanding a troop of noble cavalry and the Gascon infantry who had come with Bernardon de la Salle, had attempted to capture the Prefect di Vico near Bolsena but instead was taken prisoner himself, together with a score of laymen related to the pope and certain cardinals: Pinzi, *Storia della città di Viterbo*, 386. The prisoners were soon freed, when the Breton company of Silvestre Budes took Bolsena.

[13] Pedro Tenorio, bishop of Coimbra, promoted to Toledo; Nicola Brancaccio, archbishop of Bari, transferred to Cosenza; Bartolomeo Prignano, the deputy vice-chancellor, archbishop of Acerenza, transferred to Bari.

[14] He commanded an escort of ten lances: Mirot, *Politique*, 147.

[15] "Sicut Dei paranymphus," acting as best man in the marriage of the Curia and the City, wrote Ameilh. One document of Bertrand Raffin's quartering activity, IM 6648, is reproduced and edited by Giulio Battelli, "Gli alloggi assegnati in Roma a Raimondo di Turenne per il ritorno di Gregorio XI (1379) [better: (1377)]," in *Roma, Magistra mundi* (Louvain, 1998), 25-40. As I read this precious page, it shows Raimond and his troops

Rome to Anagni

(1) On Saturday 16 May 1377 the pope left the Vatican Palace after mass to visit S. Maria Maggiore, met by the horse guards of the bandaresi and noble marshals, escorted by the senator Gomez Albornoz and noble citizens; the squire Raimond de Turenne with his knights; the knight Hugues de la Roche, marshal of the Curia, with his barons; the knight Gui de Prohins and his followers, all in uniform, (17) also the rectors of the City and of the Sacra Societas, and the conservatores with their lawyers and sergeants. (21) The walls along Ponte S. Angelo were hung with cloth of gold, and from there to Piazza Parione with silk. At S. Maria Maggiore, a huge congregation came to the pope's mass the next morning. (37) On the 19th the pope went to his cathedral church of S. John Lateran, celebrated a single mass and returned to S. Maria Maggiore. (45) On Trinity Sunday (24 May 1377) he celebrated mass there and the people were sent home with trumpets; (49) he returned to the Lateran to say mass on Corpus Christi (28 May 1377). The people clapped their hands when the heads of Peter and Paul were shown, and the pope could not ride away, so great was the crowd. (57) He accepted petitions, gave hearing to the Jews, and granted recognition of their Mosaic Law. (61) He dined at S. Maria Maggiore with the nobles of Rome and his official family, and after dinner confirmed their friendship. After two days he departed for Anagni.

(114) When the pope departed on Saturday 30 May, Rome was so disturbed she forgot to protect him with an escort, but he went his way on muleback, offering his foot to be kissed and scattering largesse.[16] (123) His progress was disturbed by a robbery; the thief was captured and summarily hanged. (124) Over the hills in dense woods, at Grottaferrata, a convent of Greek monks, the pope stayed in the monastery with two cardinals, while four prelates with their households slept in the church. (136) As the advance baggage train departed early on 1 June, a muleteer of the bishop of Carpentras[17] was killed by an unnamed swordsman. (139) The pope left the monastery and took the Via Casilina to Anagni. After Terce the party reached the fortress of Valmontone, gateway to Campania, in the diocese of Palestrina, the pretty house of a noble lord, also citizen of Rome (the count of Valmontone and Segni). (152) They dined there and stayed the night. The next morning, 2 June, they reached Anagni before Terce. (164) Anagni has only one street, no rivers, only springs and cisterns for rain. High houses built of stones broken by earthquake, whitewashed, roofed with chestnut wood. Men and women the same dark, sunburnt color. The white wine is delicious, but

---

being assigned 15 houses and one separate stable, and seizing 5 more houses "on their own authority." Then it lists 14 other knights who were housed with their servants and squads, 3 to 13 strong.

[16] Ehrle, ed., "Chronik des ... Bertrand Boysset," 328.
[17] Pierre de Laplotte OSB, referendarius, bishop since 8 January 1376.

there is no red to be found. Fertile grain-lands, a choice region for wine, temperate climate, the people good, affable, and rustic. (176) There is a secret cavern with a spring on top of the hill, behind the church of the Virgin; many miracles have happened there. The pope was moved. He ordered a fast for 7 September (Vigil of the Nativity of the Virgin), and endowed a mass in the church, confirming the foundation with a solemn letter.

Appendix II:
Family Relations of Pope Gregory XI

Through his family relations, Pierre de Cros was involved politically and economically with the Roger clan of Gregory XI. Maintenance of the pope's relatives was a constant concern to him, as it was to the successive referendarii, who registered the petitions of privileged applicants for the best benefices.[18] Here is a summary of the Roger family tree by branches, with its marital connections to other families.

The **Aigrefeuille** family, like the Cros, were linked as cousins to the Roger by an unknown grandmother, this one a sister of Guillaume, lord of Rosiers. The cousin of Clement VI, Cardinal Guillaume d'Aigrefeuille the elder, rose by that pope's favor along with his brothers, four of whom figure in the family tree: Pierre d'Aigrefeuille, once abbot of Chaise-Dieu, who died as bishop of Avignon in 1369; Raimond d'Aigrefeuille, bishop of Rodez; Faydit d'Aigrefeuille, bishop of Avignon in succession to his brother, then cardinal under Clement VII; and Adhémar d'Aigrefeuille senior, lord of Gramat and marshal of justice of the Curia. The sons of this Adhémar were Guillaume d'Aigrefeuille the younger, created cardinal by Urban V while his uncle and namesake was still alive; Bernard d'Aigrefeuille, bishop of Viviers; and Adhémar d'Aigrefeuille junior, knight and captain of Avignon under Clement VII.[19]

We have seen that the **de Cros** connection was a sister of Clement VI. Two of that pope's brothers were Guillaume **Roger** jr, lord of Beaufort (count of Beaufort from 1347), and Hugues Roger, possibly a member of Etienne Aubert's retinue in 1338, who was appointed bishop of Tulle and then created cardinal in the

---

[18] The lines of relation to Gregory XI, as they were used to sponsor grants of benefices, were identified by Michel Hayez, "Les réserves spéciales," 242-43 (my translation): "His sister Elise, countess of Valentinois, recommended candidates through nearly the whole pontificate, and her husband Aymar de Poitiers once. Raimond de Turenne ... was more pressing than his father the viscount of Turenne, the pope's own brother. Marquis de Canilhac, half-brother of the pope, made seven recommendations, and the names of Géraud de Ventadour (lord of Donzenac, brother-in-law of the pope), Guillaume de Maumont, and Raoul de Lestrange also appear."

[19] For the Aigrefeuille, "it is difficult to state a precise degree of cousinage"; see Guillemain, *La Cour*, 120, 159, 270, 272, 436-38; Baluze-Mollat 2:415-16, 514, 689.

first year of Clement VI.[20] Hugues became chamberlain of the College of Cardinals in the plague year of 1361, and when he died in 1363 a huge cache of gold coins (the shares of common services never distributed to cardinals who had died meanwhile) was discovered in his private chests. Even before his appointment as papal chamberlain, in April 1371, Pierre de Cros was put to work on a judicial committee with Hugues, bishop of Orléans, and Guillaume de Lestrange, dean of Saintes and the pope's cubicularius. Their charge was to settle the claims by and against the executors of the testament of the late cardinal chamberlain, so that the gold found in Roger's chests could be released for use. Pierre de Cros was still at this task in 1384.[21]

The sister of Guillaume de Beaufort and Cardinal Hugues Roger, Delphine Roger, married into the **Besse** family, and her son was Nicolas de Besse, the cardinal of Limoges (1344-1369). Pierre Roger had directly supervised this nephew's education in Paris, and had placed him, it seems, among the Roger family members in the household of Etienne Aubert at the royal court in 1338.[22] As pope, Clement VI brought Nicolas to the Curia and appointed him bishop of Limoges; yet the pope declared that it was the cardinals in Consistory who forced him to make Nicolas a cardinal by refusing otherwise to assent to the promotion of Pierre Bertrand. The disclaimer was evasive: Nicolas' successor as bishop of Limoges (Guillaume de Comborn, his nephew) had been appointed more than two months before that Consistory. Delphine's daughter Elise de Besse in 1342 married Guiscard IV de **Comborn**, heir of his aunt for the lordship of Treignac. Their son Guiscard V bought the viscounty of Comborn about 1374 from a cousin, Archambaud IX, who later regretted the sale and used the title as his own.[23]

Guillemette Roger, another sister of Clement VI, married Jacques de la **Jugie** and raised the status of his family: he was knighted in 1339 and acquired the lordship of La Livinière for his son Nicolas a few years later. Two other sons became cardinals, Guillaume in 1342 and Pierre in 1375 following Guillaume's death.[24] In Pierre de Cros' letters we find another Jacques de la Jugie in the 1348 household of Guillaume de la Tissanderie, bishop of Rieux (Calendar nos. 470, 471).

---

[20] I identify Hugues Roger with entry [A 27] "Hugoni clerico" in the retinue list: Williman, "Memoranda and Sermons," 13.

[21] Baluze-Mollat 4:127-31 for the inventory of gold; EFR *Grégoire XI secrètes France*, no. 141 for the commission.

[22] I identify Nicolas de Besse with the entry [A 24] "Nicolao cappelano" in the retinue list: Williman, "Memoranda and Sermons," 13.

[23] Guillemain, *La Cour*, 203, 208; Baluze-Mollat 2:381-87; *Dictionnaire de biographie française* 9:374-75.

[24] Anne-Marie Hayez, "Une famille cardinalice à Avignon au XIVe siècle: les La Jugie," *Annuaire de la Société des amis du Palais des Papes* 57-58 (1980-1981): 25-48; Guillemain, *La Cour*, 160, 266, 272; Baluze-Mollat 2:362-67.

Another Limousin prelate whose precise connection does not appear, but who was noted as a nephew when created cardinal by Clement VI in 1342, was Adhémar **Robert**.[25] Four Roberts who may be related appear in the de Cros letters: Adhémar Robert, bishop successively of Lisieux, Arras, and Thérouanne, finally archbishop of Sens (1376-1385), served as a special papal commissioner in the spoils of Henri de Poitiers, bishop of Troyes (Calendar no. 40); Guillaume Robert in the household of Guillaume de la Tissanderie, bishop of Rieux in 1348 (Calendar nos. 470 and 471); Raimond Robert, doctor decretorum and collector of Cyprus (Calendar nos. 462 and 516); and Bertrand Robert, prior of the Benedictine convent of S. Vigor-le-Grand (Bayeux) and then of the Cluniac house of Villeneuve (Rodez) (Calendar nos. 126 and 127).

The **Lestranges** who appear in the records of Pierre de Cros were related to each other and to Gregory XI, but I have not discovered how. Guillaume de Lestrange had been dean of Saintes and a cubicularius and commensal chaplain of Gregory XI; as bishop of Carpentras (1371-1376) he represented the pope at the peace conference of Bruges, and later became archbishop of Rouen (1375-1389). Elie de Lestrange was juris utriusque doctor, dean, then bishop of Saintes (1381-1396) and bishop of Le Puy (1396-1418). Raoul de Lestrange was in the court of Gregory XI as damoiseau, then squire of honor, and he campaigned in Italy beside Raimond de Turenne in 1376-1378 and later, as a knight, parleyed for Raimond in his 1390 peace with Clement VII.[26]

The three marriages of Guillaume Roger de Beaufort, brother of Clement VI, created several more family alliances.[27] His first wife, Marie de Chambon, died while her brother-in-law Clement VI was still pope. Marie was the mother of at least ten children including Pierre Roger de Beaufort, Gregory XI, head of the family in his time. One of this pope's brothers, Jean Roger, was archbishop of Auch and then of Narbonne; another brother, Nicolas Roger, was lord of Herment and then of Limeuil. Marie's eldest child was Guillaume de Beaufort (once Beaufort became a titular county the surname Roger was seldom used), viscount of **Turenne**. Guillaume de Beaufort, heir of a name and of a county with insufficient resources to maintain his estate, married Aliénor de Comminges and sired several children of whom Raimond de Turenne and Jeanne de Beaufort will concern us most. Raimond de Turenne, sworn in as a papal damoiseau before the consecration of Gregory XI,[28] fought for the Church in the Comtat Venaissin and then in Italy and arrived at his maturity an experienced and angry warrior with his pay and honors far in arrears. Jeanne had been promised to Louis count of Forêts, but he died in the battle of Brignais. She married Raimond, lord of

---

[25] For the Robert, "cette vieille tige de l'aristocratie limousine," see Guillemain, *La Cour*, 159.

[26] Baluze-Mollat 2:675; 4:349-52; Guillemain, *La Cour*, 422.

[27] Guillemain, *La Cour*, 158-60.

[28] RA 173, 52r.

Les Baux, count of Avellino in the kingdom of Naples, and had a daughter Alix, whose rights to Les Baux and Avellino her brother Raimond de Turenne, as her guardian, took up as an excuse for war in Provence and in the Comtat-Venaissin "against a pope without a Rome (Clement VII), a king without a crown (Louis of Anjou), and a prince with no lands (Jean de Chalon, prince of Orange)."[29] After the death of Raimond des Baux, Jeanne married in 1374 Gui de Chauvigny, lord of Châteauroux in Berry and viscount of Brosse.[30]

Froissart tells the story of the three captains at the sack of Limoges who stood and fought the English princes one-on-one until they were taken prisoner.[31] Two of the three paladins belonged to the Roger clan: the squire Roger de Beaufort, son of Guillaume de Beaufort and Marie de Chambon; and the knight Jean **de la Roche**,[32] son of Marie's daughter Delphine and of Hugues de la Roche, lately a captain in the French army, later master of Gregory XI's household, who served as a captain of the Church army in Italy and from 1375 as knight marshal of the Roman Curia. It seems that both prisoners of war died unransomed, despited the efforts of Gregory XI, brother of Roger and uncle of Jean, and despite the direct pleading of Jean's father Hugues.[33] The pope extended his care to Jean's sister Delphine and to his brothers, the knight Pierre and the clerics Adhémar, Gerald, Hugues, Nicolas, and Raimond.[34]

The children of Guillaume de Beaufort's second wife Garine de **Canilhac** inherited the lordship and used the surname Canilhac, including Marquis de Canilhac and Raimond de Canilhac, who was made cardinal by Clement VI, his uncle.[35]

---

[29] Noel Valois, "Raymond de Turenne et les papes d'Avignon," *Annuaire-bulletin de la Société de l'histoire de France* 26 (1889): 215-765, here 245; Christofle Justel, *Histoire généalogique de la maison de Turene* (Paris, 1645), 66-67; Gaspard Thaumas de la Thaumassière, *Histoire de Berry* (Bourges, 1865), 2:420-21.

[30] Gui de Chauvigny survived Jeanne. She used the titles of lady of Châteauroux and viscountess of Brosse in a supplication to her uncle Gregory XI (preserved as a flyleaf of a manuscript in Reims) asking benefices for several clerics: *Catalogue général des manuscrits des bibliothèques publiques de France*, vol. 39, 158-59.

[31] Froissart, *Chroniques*, ed. Kervyn, 8:42; trans. Berners, 2:356, chap. 283.

[32] Froissart erroneously gave him his father's name, Hugues.

[33] Guillemain, *La Cour*, 172-73; and see Calendar Appendix A6 and A7 on the enclosed compact disk.

[34] VQ 6:359 and 512; cf. Calendar no. 644; Baluze-Mollat 2:340-41. The younger Hugues de la Roche, archdeacon of Fenouillèdes and therefore lord of the castle of Arsan, needed a direct pardon from Louis duke of Anjou in February 1376 (style of France, 1375) because the governor of the castle had disobeyed the king's order to improve the fortifications or to destroy the castle, "après que la place eut été escaladée, prise et brulée par les compagnies": Devic and Vaissete, *Histoire générale de Languedoc*, 9:846.

[35] Baluze-Mollat 2:406.

Guillaume de Beaufort's third wife Catherine **de la Garde** had only one child, Raimond de Beaufort, viscount of Valernes, who died in 1420 and was buried in the College of S. Martial, in the chapel dedicated by his uncle Pierre de Cros to the memory of the Roger popes.[36]

Various clerics named de Turre may have been connected to Guillaume de **la Tour** who married Gregory XI's sister Marthe; but the closest was the cardinal Bernard de la Tour (1342-1361), Guillaume's uncle. The cardinal Jean de la Tour (1371-1374) was from another family entirely.[37]

---

[36] Baluze-Mollat 2:339; Léopold Duhamel, "Le tombeau de Raymond de Beaufort à St-Martial d'Avignon," *Mémoires de l'Academie de Vaucluse* 2 (1883): 1-14.

[37] Baluze-Mollat 2:361-62, 615.

Select Genealogy: Roger and Allied Families

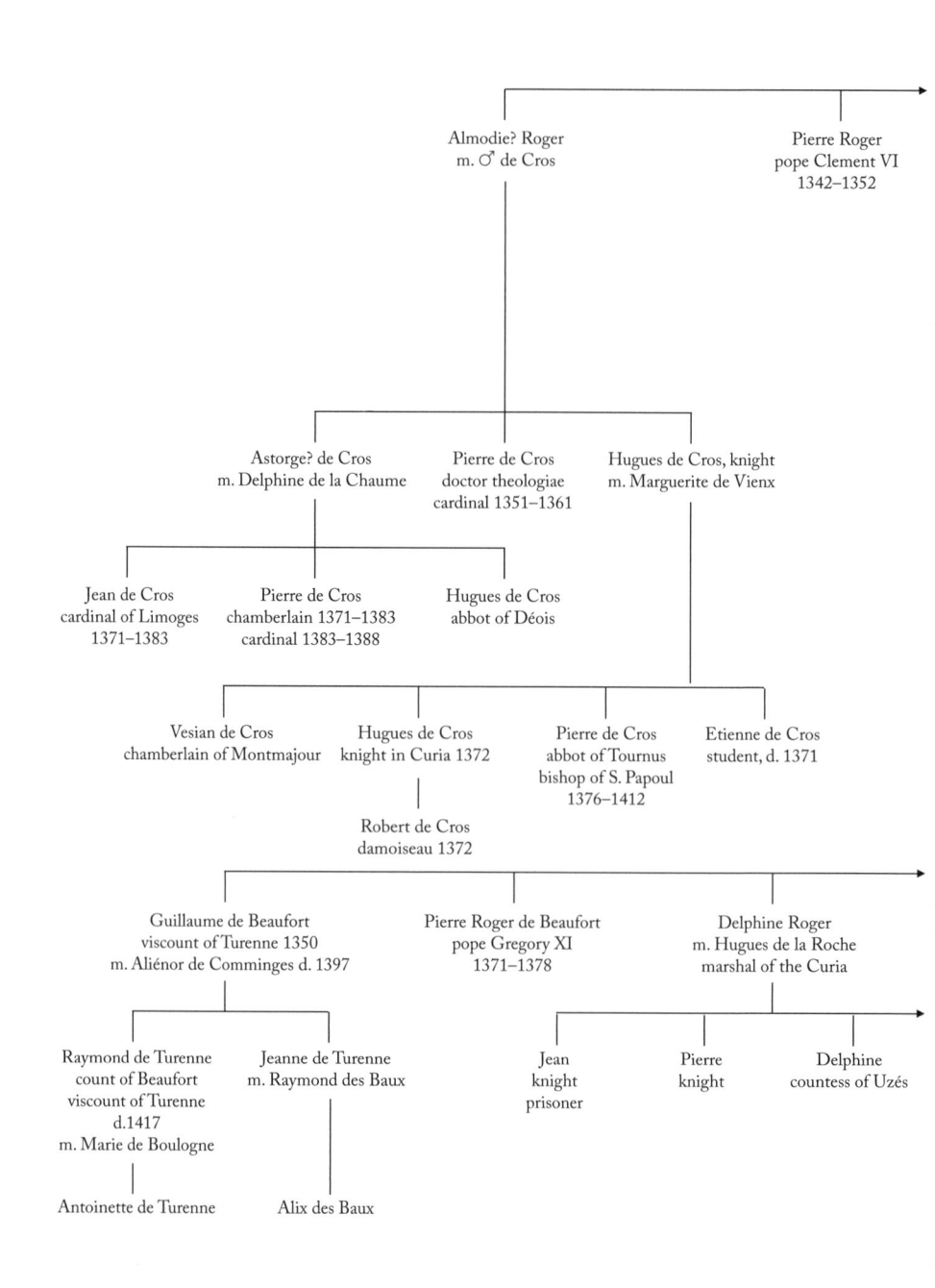

- Almodie? Roger m. ♂ de Cros
  - Astorge? de Cros m. Delphine de la Chaume
    - Jean de Cros, cardinal of Limoges 1371–1383
    - Pierre de Cros, chamberlain 1371–1383, cardinal 1383–1388
    - Hugues de Cros, abbot of Déois
  - Pierre de Cros, doctor theologiae, cardinal 1351–1361
  - Hugues de Cros, knight, m. Marguerite de Vienx
    - Vesian de Cros, chamberlain of Montmajour
    - Hugues de Cros, knight in Curia 1372
      - Robert de Cros, damoiseau 1372
    - Pierre de Cros, abbot of Tournus, bishop of S. Papoul 1376–1412
    - Etienne de Cros, student, d. 1371
- Pierre Roger, pope Clement VI 1342–1352
  - Guillaume de Beaufort, viscount of Turenne 1350, m. Aliénor de Comminges d. 1397
    - Raymond de Turenne, count of Beaufort, viscount of Turenne, d.1417, m. Marie de Boulogne
      - Antoinette de Turenne
    - Jeanne de Turenne m. Raymond des Baux
      - Alix des Baux
  - Pierre Roger de Beaufort, pope Gregory XI 1371–1378
  - Delphine Roger m. Hugues de la Roche, marshal of the Curia
    - Jean, knight, prisoner
    - Pierre, knight
    - Delphine, countess of Uzés

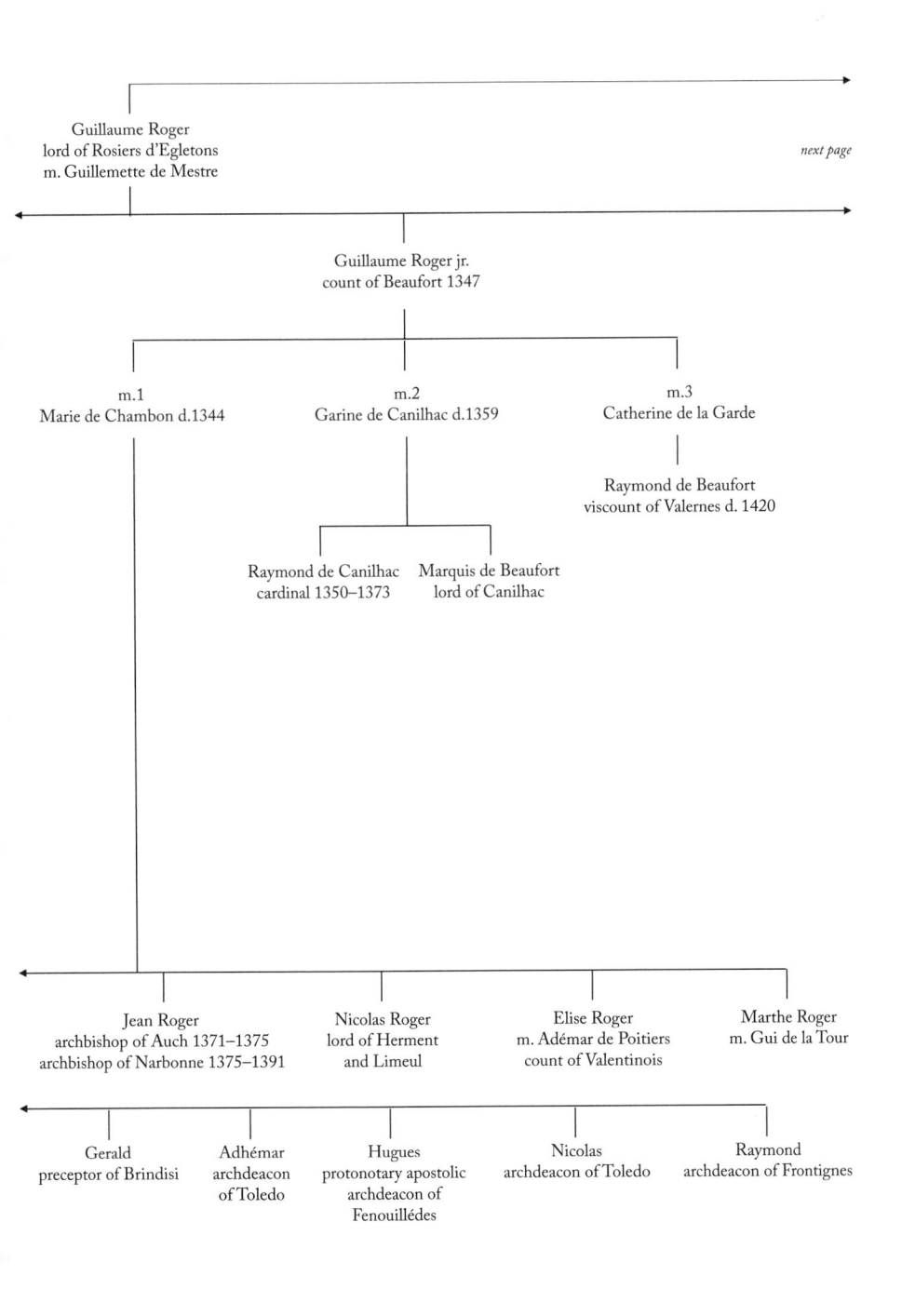

Guillaume Roger
lord of Rosiers d'Egletons
m. Guillemette de Mestre

next page

Guillaume Roger jr.
count of Beaufort 1347

m.1
Marie de Chambon d.1344

m.2
Garine de Canilhac d.1359

m.3
Catherine de la Garde

Raymond de Beaufort
viscount of Valernes d. 1420

Raymond de Canilhac
cardinal 1350–1373

Marquis de Beaufort
lord of Canilhac

Jean Roger
archbishop of Auch 1371–1375
archbishop of Narbonne 1375–1391

Nicolas Roger
lord of Herment
and Limeul

Elise Roger
m. Adémar de Poitiers
count of Valentinois

Marthe Roger
m. Gui de la Tour

Gerald
preceptor of Brindisi

Adhémar
archdeacon
of Toledo

Hugues
protonotary apostolic
archdeacon of
Fenouillédes

Nicolas
archdeacon of Toledo

Raymond
archdeacon of Frontignes

Select Genealogy: Roger and Allied Families *(continued)*

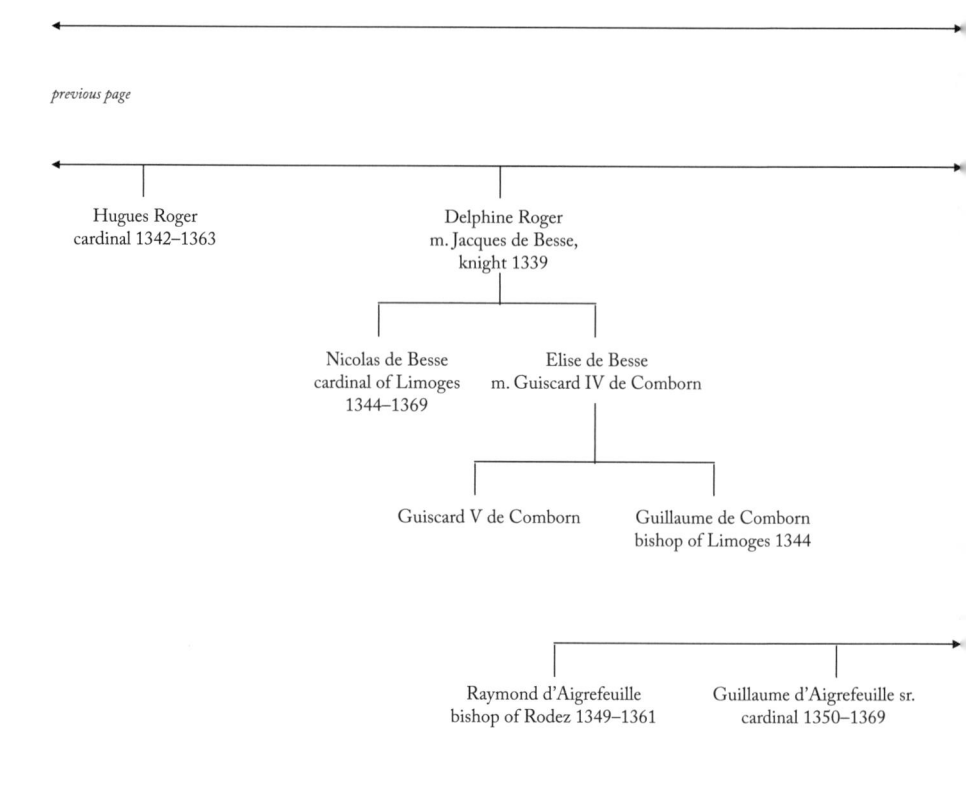

previous page

- Hugues Roger
  cardinal 1342–1363
- Delphine Roger
  m. Jacques de Besse, knight 1339
  - Nicolas de Besse
    cardinal of Limoges
    1344–1369
  - Elise de Besse
    m. Guiscard IV de Comborn
    - Guiscard V de Comborn
    - Guillaume de Comborn
      bishop of Limoges 1344
      - Raymond d'Aigrefeuille
        bishop of Rodez 1349–1361
      - Guillaume d'Aigrefeuille sr.
        cardinal 1350–1369
        - Guillaume d'Aigrefeuille jr
          cardinal 1367–1401

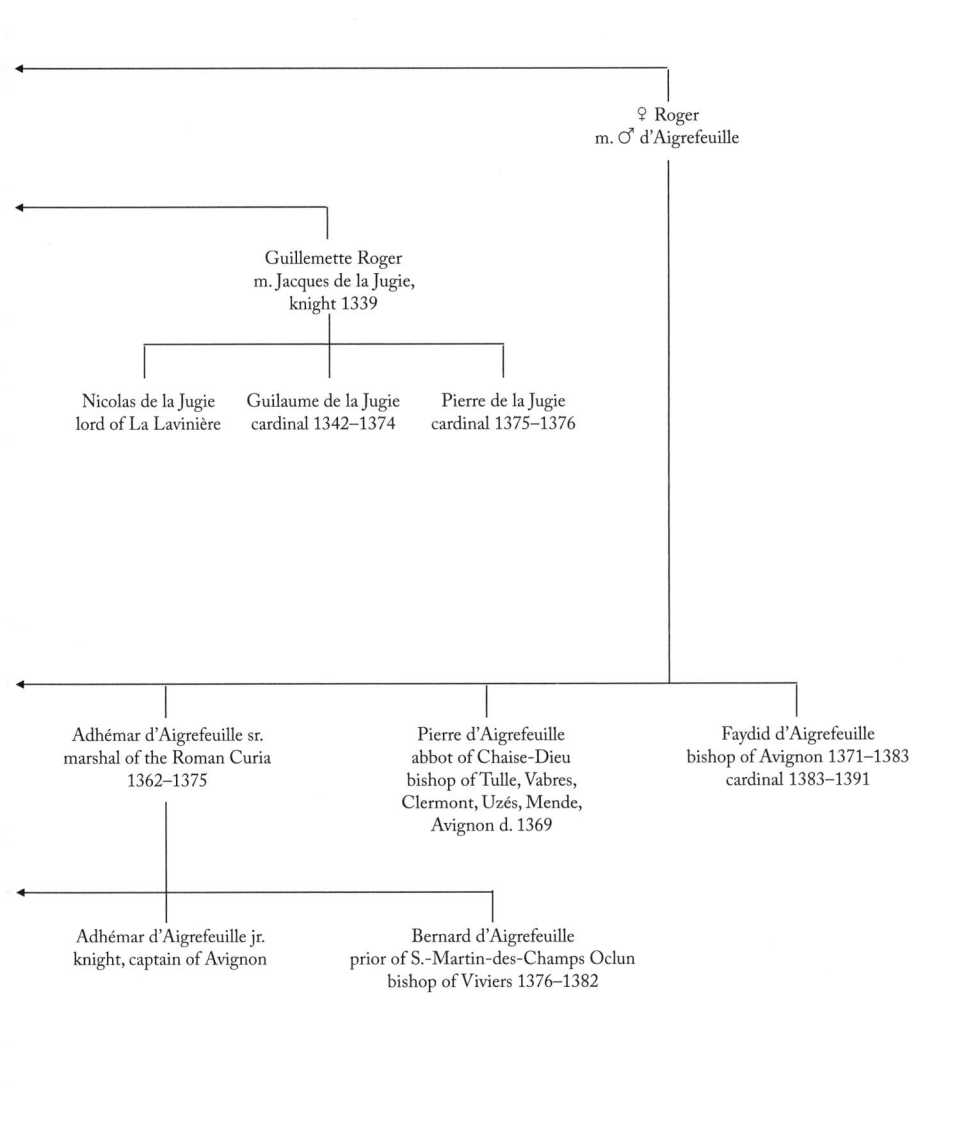

♀ Roger
m. ♂ d'Aigrefeuille

Guillemette Roger
m. Jacques de la Jugie,
knight 1339

Nicolas de la Jugie
lord of La Lavinière

Guilaume de la Jugie
cardinal 1342–1374

Pierre de la Jugie
cardinal 1375–1376

Adhémar d'Aigrefeuille sr.
marshal of the Roman Curia
1362–1375

Pierre d'Aigrefeuille
abbot of Chaise-Dieu
bishop of Tulle, Vabres,
Clermont, Uzés, Mende,
Avignon d. 1369

Faydid d'Aigrefeuille
bishop of Avignon 1371–1383
cardinal 1383–1391

Adhémar d'Aigrefeuille jr.
knight, captain of Avignon

Bernard d'Aigrefeuille
prior of S.-Martin-des-Champs Oclun
bishop of Viviers 1376–1382

Bibliography

A. Published Sources, Guides, Bibliographies

Achard, Félix [better: Paul], and Léopold Duhamel, eds. *Inventaire sommaire des Archives communales d'Avignon.* Avignon, 1863–1953.

Achery, Luc d'. *Spicilegium sive collectio veterum aliquot scriptorum qui in Galliae bibliothecis delituerant.* 13 vols.: Paris, 1655–1677; 3 vols.: Paris, 1723.

Acta pontificum danica. 1: 1316–1378 (Det avignonske tidsrum), ed. L. Maltesen. Copenhagen, 1904; 7: *Supplementum,* ed. Alfred Krarup. Copenhagen, 1943.

Albanès, Joseph Mathias Hyacinthe. *Gallia Christiana Novissima.* 7 vols.; Montbéliard, 1899–1920. 1. *Aix* (1899); 2. *Marseille* (1899); 3. *Arles* (1901); 4. *S.-Paul-trois-châteaux* (1909); 5. *Toulon* (1911); 6. *Orange* (1916); 7. *Avignon* (1920).

Analecta Vaticano-Belgica: Documents relatifs aux anciens diocèses de Cambrai, Liège, Thérouanne et Tournai. Institut historique belge de Rome, 10: *Les Collectories pontificales dans les anciens diocèses au XIVe siècle.* Ed. Ursmer Berlière. Rome, 1929.

Annales ecclesiastici denuo excusi et ad nostra tempora perducti. Ed. Cesare Baronio et al., and Agostino Theiner. Vol. 26: *1356–1396.* Paris, 1872.

Arias, Gino. "La chiesa e la storia economica del Medio Evo." *Archivio della Reale Società di Storia Patria* 29 (1906): 145–81.

Bååth, L. M. *Diplomatarium Svecanum,* appendix: *Acta pontificum suecica* 1: *Acta cameralia,* vol. 1, fasc. 2. Stockholm, 1942.

Baluze, Etienne. *Vitae paparum avenionensium.* Ed. Guillaume Mollat. 4 vols. Paris, 1914–1927. 1. *Vitae* with index; 2. *Notae ad Vitas* with index; 3–4. *Collectio actorum veterum* and index.

Barbiche, Bernard. *Les actes pontificaux originaux des Archives nationales de Paris* 3: *1305–1415.* Index actorum Romanorum Pontificum ab Innocentio III ad Martinum V electum III. Vatican City, 1982.

Battelli, Giulio. "Gli alloggi assegnati in Roma a Raimondo di Turenne per il ritorno di Gregorio XI (1379)[better: 1377]." In *Roma, Magistra mundi:*

Itineraria culturae medievalis: Mélanges offerts au Père L. E. Boyle à l'occasion de son 75e anniversaire, 25–40. Louvain, 1998.

Baumgarten, Paul Maria. *Aus Kanzlei und Kammer: Erörtungen zur Kurialen Hof- und Verwaltungsgeschichte im XII., XIV. und XV. Jahrhundert: Bullatores, taxatores domorum, cursores*. Freiburg im Breisgau, 1907.

———. *Untersuchungen und Urkunden über die Camera Collegii Cardinalium für die Zeit von 1295 bis 1437*. Leipzig, 1898.

Bautier, Robert-Henri, and Janine Sornay. *Les sources de l'histoire économique et sociale du moyen âge*, 1: *Provence-Comtat Venaissin-Dauphiné-Etats de la maison de Savoie*. 3 vols. Paris, 1968–1974.

Berman, Allen G. *Papal Coins*. South Salem, NY, 1991.

Bibliografia dell'Archivio Vaticano. 9 vols. to date. Vatican City, 1962–2003.

Birch, Walter de Grey, ed. "*Vita Sanctissimi Martialis Apostoli*: The Life of St. Martial by Aurelianus, from a Manuscript in the British Museum." *Journal of the British Archaeological Association* 28 (1872): 353–90.

Böhmer, Johann Friedrich, ed. *Die Regesten des Kaiserreichs unter Kaiser Karl IV, 1346–1378*. Regesta Imperii 8. Innsbruck, 1877; repr. 1967.

Bonazzi, Luigi. *Storia di Perugia dalle origine al 1860*. 2 vols.; 1: *Dalle origine al 1494*. Perugia, 1875.

Bresc, Henri, ed. *La correspondence de Pierre Ameilh, archevêque de Naples, puis d'Embrun (1363–1369)*. Paris, 1972.

Bullarum, diplomatum et privilegiorum sanctorum Romanorum Pontificum Taurinensis editio. 25 vols. Turin, 1857–1885.

Bussi, Feliciano. *Istoria della città di Viterbo*. Rome, 1742; repr. Bologna, 1967.

Chevalier, Ulysse. *Repertoire des sources historiques du moyen âge: Bio-bibliographie*. 2 vols. Paris, 1905–1907; repr. New York, 1960. *Topo-bibliographie*. 2 vols. Paris, 1905; repr. New York, 1959.

Ciampi, Ignazio, ed. *Niccola della Tuccia, Cronaca di Viterbo*, part 1 (*1095–1476*). In *Chronache e statuti della città di Viterbo*, 3–112, 277–410. Documenti di storia italiana pubblicati a cura della Reale deputazione sugli studi di storia patria per le provincie di Toscana, dell'Umbria et delle Marche 5. Florence, 1872.

Codex Italiae diplomaticus. Ed. Johann Christian Lünig. 4 vols. Frankfurt and Leipzig, 1732.

Corpus iuris canonici. Ed. Aemilianus Friedberg. 2d ed. 2 vols. 1. *Decretum magistri Gratiani*; 2. *Decretalium collectiones*. Leipzig, 1879–1881; repr. Graz, 1955.

Delachenal, Robert, ed. *Chronique des règnes de Jean II et de Charles V*. 4 vols. Société de l'histoire de France. Paris, 1910–1920.

Delisle, Léopold, ed. *Mandements et actes divers de Charles V (1364–1380)*. Collection de documents inédits sur l'histoire de France, sér. 1: Histoire politique. Paris, 1874.

Diplomatarium Danicum 3: 9 *(1371–1375)*. Copenhagen, 1982.

Dictionnaire de biographie française. 20 vols. to date. Paris, 1933–2004.

Dictionnaire d'histoire et de géographie ecclésiastiques. 29 vols. to date. Paris, 1912–2006.

Dizionario biografico degli Italiani. 60 vols. published to date. Rome, 1960–2006.

Duprè Theseider, Eugenio. "La rivolta di Perugia nel 1375 contro l'abate di Monmaggiore [sic] ed i suoi precedenti politici." *Bolletino della Reale deputazione di storia patria per l'Umbria* 35 (1938): 69–166.

Ecoles françaises d'Athènes et de Rome, Bibliothèque, 3e série: Lettres communes des papes du XIVe siècle: *Grégoire XI (1370–1378): Lettres communes, analysées d'après les registres dits d'Avignon et du Vatican*. Ed. Anne-Marie Hayez. 3 vols. published to date. Rome, 1992- .

———: *Lettres secrètes et curiales du pape Grégoire XI (1370–1378) intéressant les pays autres que la France, publiées ou analysées d'après les registres du Vatican*. Ed. Guillaume Mollat. 3 fasc. Paris, 1962–1965.

———: *Lettres secrètes et curiales du pape Grégoire XI (1370–1378) relatives à la France extraites des registres du Vatican*. Ed. L. Mirot and L. Jassemin. 5 fasc. Paris, 1935–1957.

———: *Urbain V (1362–1370:) Lettres communes, analysées d'après les registres dits d'Avignon et du Vatican*. 9 vols. registers, 3 vols. index. Paris, 1954–1989.

Ehrle, Franz, ed. "Die Chronik des Garoscus de Ulmoisca Veteri und Bertrand Boysset." *Archiv für Literatur- und Kulturgeschichte des Mittelalters* 7 (1893–1900): 311–420.

Ennen, Leonard, ed. *Quellen zur Geschichte der Stadt Köln* 5. Cologne, 1875; repr. Aalen, 1970.

Eubel, Conrad. *Hierarchia catholica medii aevi* vol. 1: *1198–1431*. 2d ed. Regensburg, 1915; repr. Padua, 1960.

Fasti ecclesiae Anglicanae 1300–1541. Ed. John Le Neve. 12 vols., various compilers. London, 1962–1967. 1. *Lincoln Diocese*; 2. *Hereford Diocese*; 3. *Salisbury Diocese*; 4. *Monastic Cathedrals*; 5. *St. Paul's, London*; 6. *Northern Province*; 7. *Chichester Diocese*; 8. *Bath and Wells Diocese*; 9. *Exeter Diocese*; 10. *Coventry and Lichfield Diocese*; 11. *The Welsh Dioceses*; 12. *Introduction, Errata and index*.

Fasti ecclesiae Gallicanae: Répertoire prosopographique des évêques, dignitaires et chanoines de France de 1200 à 1500. Directed by Hélène Millet. Turnhout, 1996- . 1. *Diocèse d'Amiens*; 2. *Diocèse de Rouen*; 3. *Diocèse de Reims*; 4.

Diocèse de Besançon; 5. *Diocèse d'Agen*; 6. *Diocèse de Rodez*; 7. *Diocèse d'Angers*; 8. *Diocèse de Mende*; 9. *Diocèse de Sées*.

Froissart, Jean. *Oeuvres de Froissart: Chroniques*. Ed. Kervyn de Lettenhove. 25 vols. in 26. Brussels, 1867–1877.

———. *The Chronicles of England, France, Spain, and other places adjoining*. Trans. John Bourchier, Lord Berners. Intro. William Paton Ker. 6 vols. London, 1901–1903.

Gallia Christiana in provincias ecclesiasticas distributa. Ed. Paul Piolin. 2d ed. Rome and Paris, 1870.

Glénisson, Jean, ed. *L'enquête pontificale de 1373 sur l'Ordre des Hospitaliers de S. Jean de Jérusalem*. 1: A.-M. Legras and R. Favreau, *L'enquête dans le Prieuré de France*. Paris, 1987.

Hoberg, Hermann. *Die Inventare des päpstlichen Schatzes in Avignon, 1314–1376*. Studi e Testi 111. Vatican City, 1944.

Kirsch, Johann Peter. *Die päpstlichen Kollektorien in Deutschland während des XIV. Jahrhunderts*. Quellen und Forschungen aus dem Gebiete der Geschichte 3. Paderborn, 1894.

———. *Die Rückkehr der Päpste Urban V. und Gregor XI. von Avignon nach Rom: Auszüge aus den Kameralregistern des Vatikanischen Archivs*. Quellen und Forschungen aus dem Gebiete der Geschichte 6. Paderborn, 1898.

Lexikon des Mittelalters. 9 vols. Munich, 2003.

Lunt, William E. *Accounts Rendered by Papal Collectors in England, 1317–1378*. Rev. ed. Edgar B. Graves. Memoirs of the American Philosophical Society 70. Philadelphia, 1968.

Mannucci, Ubaldo. "Lettere di Collettori pontifici nel secolo XIV." *Römische Quartalschrift für christliche Altertumskunde und für Kirchengeschichte* 27 (1913): 190*-201*.

Masai, François. "Principes et conventions de l'édition diplomatique." *Scriptorium* 4 (1950): 190–93.

Osio, Luigi, ed. *Documenti diplomatici tratti dagli archivi milanesi*. 3 vols. Milan, 1864–1872.

Ottenthal, Emil von, ed. *Regulae cancellariae apostolicae: Die päpstlichen Kanzleiregeln von Johannes XXII bis Nicolaus V.* Innsbruck, 1888; repr. Aalen, 1968.

Pavelige Aktatykker vedrørende Danmark 1: *1316–1378 (Det avignonske Tidsrum)*. Ed. L. Moltesen. Copenhagen, 1904.

Pinzi, Cesare. *Storia della città di Viterbo*. 4 vols. Rome, 1887–1889; Viterbo, 1899–1913; repr. Viterbo, 1969, Rome, 1974.

Poey d'Avant, Faustin. *Monnaies féodales de France*. 4 vols. Paris, 1858–1862.

Ptaśnik, Joannes, ed. *Monumenta Poloniae Vaticana* 1–2: *Acta Camerae apostolicae.* 2 vols. Vol. 2: *1344–1374.* Cracow, 1913.

Muratori, Ludovico Antonio, ed. *Rerum italicarum scriptores.* 25 vols. Milan, 1723–1751.

Ronzy, Pierre. *Le voyage de Grégoire XI ramenant la papauté d'Avignon à Rome (1376–1377) suivi du texte latin et de la traduction française de l'*Itinerarium Gregorii XI *de Pierre Ameilh.* Publications de l'Institut français de Florence. Florence, 1952.

Sacchetti, Franco. *Il trecentonovelle.* Ed. Vincenzo Pernicone. Florence, 1946.

Samaran, Charles. "La jurisprudence pontificale en matière de droit de dépouille *(jus spolii)* dans la second moitié du XIVe siècle." *Mélanges d'archéologie et d'histoire* 22 (1902): 141-56.

———, and Guillaume Mollat. *La fiscalité pontificale en France au XIVe siècle.* Bibliothèque des Ecoles françaises d'Athènes et de Rome 96. Paris, 1905.

Sauerland, Heinrich V., ed. *Urkunden und Regesten zur Geschichte der Rheinlande aus dem Vatikanischen Archiv* 5: *1362–1378.* Bonn, 1910.

Schäfer, Karl Heinrich. *Die Ausgaben der apostolischen Kammer unter den Päpsten Urban V und Gregor XI (1362–1378).* Vatikanische Quellen 6. Paderborn, 1937.

———. "Wertvergleiche des Florentiner Goldguldens zu den Edelmetallen und den wichtigsten europäischen Gold-, Silber- und Scheidemünzen im 13. und 14. Jahrhundert." In *Vatikanische Quellen* 2, 38*-131*. Paderborn, 1912

Segrè, Arturo, ed. "I dispacci di Cristoforo da Piacenza, procuratore mantovano alla corte pontificale (1371–1383)." *Archivio storico italiano* ser. 5, 43 (1909): 27–95; 44 (1909): 253–326.

Sella, Pietro, and M.-H. Laurent. *I sigilli dell'Archivio segreto vaticano.* 3 vols. Vatican City, 1937, 1946, 1964.

Serafini, Camillo. *Le monete e le bolle plombee pontificie del Medagliere Vaticano.* 4 vols. Milan, 1910–1928.

Spufford, Peter. *Handbook of Medieval Exchange.* London, 1986.

Tautù, A. L. *Acta Gregorii P. P. XI (1370–1378) e Regestis Vaticanis aliisque fontibus.* Pontificia commissio ad redigendum codicem iuris canonici orientalis: fontes, ser. 3, 12. Rome, 1966.

Theiner, Augustin. *Codex diplomaticus dominii temporalis S. Sedis: Recueil de documents pour servir à l'histoire du gouvernement temporel des états du Saint-Siège, extraits des archives du Vatican.* 3 vols. Vol. 2: *1335–1389.* Rome, 1861–1862; repr. Frankfurt, 1964.

Wauchier de Denain. *La Vie Seint Marcel de Lymoges.* Ed. Molly Lynde-Recchia. Geneva, 2005.

Weiss, Stefan. *Rechnungswesen und Buchhaltung des Avignoneser Papsttums (1316–1378): Eine Quellenkunde.* Monumenta Germaniae Historica, Hilfsmittel 20. Hannover, 2003.

———. *Die Versorgung des päpstlichen Hofes in Avignon mit Lebensmitteln (1316–1378): Studien zur Sozial- und Wirtschaftsgeschichte eines mittelalterlichen Hofes.* Berlin, 2002.

Williman, Daniel. *Bibliothèques ecclésiastiques au temps de la papauté d'Avignon* I: *I. Inventaires de bibliothèques et mentions de livres dans les Archives du Vatican (1287–1420) -- Répertoire*; II. *Inventaires de prélats et de clercs non français—Edition.* Paris, 1980.

———. *Calendar of the Letters of Arnaud Aubert, Camerarius Apostolicus (1361–1371).* Subsidia Mediaevalia 20. Toronto, 1992.

———. "Letters of Etienne Cambarou, Camerarius Apostolicus (1347–1361)." *Archivum Historiae Pontificiae* 15 (1977): 195–215.

———. "Memoranda and Sermons of Etienne Aubert (Innocent VI) as Bishop (1338–1341)." *Mediaeval Studies* 37 (1975): 7–41.

———. *The Right of Spoil of the Popes of Avignon 1316–1415.* Transactions of the American Philosophical Society 78.6. Philadelphia, 1988.

———. "A Sad Moment for Official Rhetoric." *General Linguistics* 35 (1995): 177–80.

———, and Karen Corsano. "The Interdict of Florence (31 March 1376): New Documents." *Rivista di Storia della Chiesa in Italia* 56 (2002): 427–81.

———, with Karen Corsano and Anne-Marie Hayez. "Les Statuts de la Cour Temporelle d'Avignon en 1375." *Mémoires de l'Académie de Vaucluse*, 8e série, 8 (1999): 9–27.

Zupko, R. E. *French Weights and Measures Before the Revolution: A Dictionary of Provincial and Local Units.* Bloomington, 1978.

B. Secondary Works

André-Michel, Robert. "La défense d'Avignon sous Urbain V et Grégoire XI." *Mélanges d'archéologie et d'histoire* 30 (1910): 129–45.

Aux origines de l'état moderne: Le fonctionnement administratif de la papauté d'Avignon. Actes de la table ronde organisée par l'Ecole française de Rome avec le concours du CNRS, du Conseil général de Vaucluse et de l'Université d'Avignon (Avignon, 23–24 janvier 1988). Collection de l'Ecole francaise de Rome 138. Rome, 1990.

Baix, Francois. "Notes sur les clercs de la Chambre apostolique (13e-14e siècles)." *Bulletin de l'Institut historique belge de Rome* 27 (1952): 17–52.

Becquet, J. "La fondation du chapitre S.-Germain près Masseret par le cardinal de Tulle [Hugo Rogerii] (XIVe siècle)." *Lemouzi* 65 (1985): 239–43.

Chiffoleau, Jacques. *Les justices du Pape: délinquance et criminalité dans la région d'Avignon au XIVe siècle.* Paris, 1984.

Cingria, Hélène, et al. *La Chartreuse du Val de Bénédiction, Villeneuve-lès-Avignon.* Paris, 1977.

Colombe, Gabriel. "La 'Grande trésorerie' au Palais apostolique d'Avignon." In *Miscellanea Francesco Ehrle*, 2:504–23. Studi e Testi 38. Vatican City, 1924.

Davies, Richard G. "The Anglo-papal Concordat of Bruges, 1375: A Reconsideration." *Archivum historiae pontificiae* 19 (1981): 97–146.

Denifle, Henri. *La désolation des églises, monastères et hopitaux en France pendant la Guerre de Cent Ans.* 2 vols. Paris, 1899.

Devic, Claude, and Joseph Vaissete. *Histoire générale de Languedoc, avec des notes et les pièces justificatives.* Ed. Auguste Molinier et al. 16 vols. Toulouse, 1872–1904. Vol. 9: *1271–1443.* Toulouse, 1885.

Duhamel, Léopold. "Le tombeau de Raymond de Beaufort à St-Martial d'Avignon." *Mémoires de l'Academie du Vaucluse* 2 (1883): 1–14.

Dykmans, Marc. "La bulle de Grégoire XI à la veille du Grand Schisme." *Mélanges d'archéologie et d'histoire* 89 (1977): 485–95.

———. "Clemente VII antipapa." In *Dizionario biografico degli Italiani* 26 (1982), 222–37.

———. "La fin du séjour des papes en Avignon d'après quelques documents inédits sur les habitations." *Mémoires de l'Académie de Vaucluse*, 7e sér., 4 (1983): 17–53.

Elzière, Jean-Bernard. *Histoire des Budos, seigneurs de Budos en Guyenne et de Portes-Bertrand en Languedoc.* Portes, 1978.

Faure, Claude. *Etude sur l'administration et l'histoire du Comtat-Venaissin du XIIIe au XVe siècle (1229–1417).* Recherches historiques et documents sur Avignon, le Comtat-Venaissin et la principauté d'Orange 3. Paris and Avignon, 1909.

Favier, Jean. *Les finances pontificales à l'époque du Grand Schisme d'Occident (1378–1409).* Bibliothèques des Ecoles françaises d'Athènes et de Rome 211. Paris, 1966.

———. "Finances pontificales: XIIIe-XVe siècles." In *Dictionnaire historique de la papauté*, 683–87. Paris, 1994.

———. "Les galées de Louis d'Anjou." In *Horizons marins, itinéraires spirituels (Ve-XVIIIe siècles)*, ed. Henri Dubois et al., vol. 2, *Marins, navires et affaires*, 137–46. Paris, 1987.

Fournier, Marcel. "Une Enquête dans un collège de droit de l'université de Montpellier au XIVe siècle." *Revue internationale d'enseignement* 17 (1889): 278–91.

Fowler, Kenneth. *Medieval Mercenaries* 1: *The Great Companies*. Oxford, 2001.

Gagnière, Sylvain. "Le Trésor bas dans la Tour du Pape: fouilles et restauration." *Annuaire de la Société des Amis du Palais des Papes* 71–72 (1984–1985): 45–65.

Galland, Bruno. *Les papes d'Avignon et la maison de Savoie (1309–1409)*. Collection de l'Ecole française de Rome 247. Rome, 1998.

———. "Le rôle du comte de Savoie dans la 'ligue' de Grégoire XI contre les Visconti (1372–1375)." *Mélanges de l'Ecole française de Rome: Moyen âge* 105 (1993): 763–823.

Gane, Robert. *Le chapitre de Notre-Dame de Paris au XIVe s.: Etude sociale d'un groupe canonial*. Ed. Claudine Billot. Saint-Etienne, 1999.

Genèse et débuts du Grand Schisme d'Occident: Avignon 25–28 septembre 1978. Colloques internationaux du Centre national de la recherche scientifique 586. Paris, 1980.

Girard, Joseph, and Pierre Pansier. *La Cour temporelle d'Avignon aux XIVme et XVme siècles: contribution à l'étude des institutions judiciaires, administratives et économiques de la ville d'Avignon au moyen âge*. Paris, 1909.

Glénisson, Jean. "Un agent de la Chambre apostolique au XIVe siècle: Les missions de Bertrand du Mazel (1364–1378)." *Mélanges d'archéologie et d'histoire* 59 (1947): 89–119.

———. "Les origines de la révolte de l'Etat pontifical en 1375." *Rivista di Storia della Chiesa in Italia* 5 (1951): 145–68.

Göller, Emil. *Die päpstliche Pönitentiarie von ihrem Ursprung bis zu ihrer Umgestaltung unter Pius V*. 2 vols. Rome, 1907–1911.

Greiner, Lily. "Un représentant de la Chambre apostolique de Clément VII en Aragon au début du Grand Schisme (1378–1380)." *Mélanges d'archéologie et d'histoire* 65 (1953): 197–214.

Guillemain, Bernard. *La Cour pontificale d'Avignon (1309–1376): Etude d'une société*. 2nd ed. Paris, 1966.

———. "Les tribunaux de la cour pontificale d'Avignon." In *L'Eglise et le droit dans le Midi (XIIIe-XIVe s.)*, 339–60. Cahiers de Fanjeaux 29. Toulouse, 1994.

Harvey, Margaret. "The Household of Simon Langham." *Journal of Ecclesiastical History* 47 (1996): 18–44.

Hayez, Anne-Marie. "Un aperçu de la politique bénéficiale de Grégoire XI." In *Forschungen zur Reichs-, Papst- und Landesgeschichte: Peter Herde zum 65. Geburtstag von Freunden, Schülern und Kollegen dargebracht*, ed. Karl Borchardt and Enno Bünz, 2:685–98. Stuttgart, 1998.

———. "Avignon, son seigneur et son conseil au XIVe siècle." *Mémoires de l'Académie de Vaucluse*, 8e série, 6 (1997): 37–60.

———. "Une famille cardinalice à Avignon au XIVe siècle: les La Jugie." *Annuaire de la Société des amis du Palais des Papes* 57–58 (1980–1981): 25–48.

———. "Les livrées avignonnaises de la période pontificale." *Mémoires de l'Académie de Vaucluse*, 8e série, 1 (1992): 93–130; 2 (1993): 15–57; 3 (1994): 33–89 with indices.

———. "Le patrimoine urbain d'un marchand cordier avignonnais, Jean Teisseire (+1384)." *Bibliothèque de l'Ecole des Chartes* 154 (1996): 427–84.

Hayez, Michel. "Avignon sans les papes." In *Genèse et débuts du Grand Schisme d'Occident*, 143–57.

———. "Les réserves spéciales de bénéfices sous Urbain V et Grégoire XI." In *Aux origines de l'état moderne*, 237–49.

Justel, Christofle. *Histoire généalogique de la maison de Turene: justifiée par chartes, titres et histoires anciennes, et autres preuves authentiques, enrichie de plusieurs seaux, et armoiries, et divisée en deux Livres*. Paris, 1645.

Kaminsky, Howard. "The Great Schism." In *The New Cambridge Medieval History*, vol. 6: *c. 1300 - c. 1415*, 674–96. Cambridge, 2000.

Labande, Léon-Honoré. *Le palais des papes et les monuments d'Avignon au XIVe siècle*. 2 vols. Marseille and Aix-en-Provence, 1925.

Lentsch, Roberte. "La localisation et l'organisation matérielle des services administratifs au palais des Papes." In *Aux origines de l'état moderne*, 293–312.

Lucarelli, Giuliano. *I Visconti di Milano e Lucca risorta a stato autonomo*. Ed. Michele Luzzati. Lucca, 1984.

Lunt, William E. *Papal Revenues in the Middle Ages*. 2 vols. Records of Civilization 19. New York, 1934.

Mazzaoui, Maureen Fennell. *The Italian Cotton Industry in the Later Middle Ages, 1100–1600*. Cambridge, 1981.

Merceron, Pierrette and Robert. "Retour de la papauté à Rome: Six-centième anniversaire, 1377–1977, Le Grand Schisme." *Lemouzi* 57 (1977): 40–50.

———, and Hervé Aliquot. "Armorial des cardinaux limousins de la papauté d'Avignon." *Lemouzi* 60 (1980): 276–99, 374–411; 61 (1981): 43–65, 177–203, 259–76, 357–80; 62 (1982): 33–59, 173–83.

Mirot, Léon. *La politique pontificale et le retour du Saint-Siège à Rome en 1376*. Paris, 1899.

———. "Les rapports financiers de Grégoire XI et du duc d'Anjou." *Mélanges d'archéologie et d'histoire* 17 (1897): 113–44.

Mitis, Oscar von. "Curiale Eidregister: Zwei Amtsbücher aus der Kammer Martins V." *Mitteilungen des Instituts für österreichischen Geschichtsforschung*, Ergänzungsband 6, 413–48. Innsbrück, 1901.

Mollat, Guillaume. "Cros (Jean de)." *DHGE* 13 (1956), cols. 1064–1065.

———. *Les papes d'Avignon (1305–1378)*. 10th ed. Paris, 1964.

Müntz, Eugène. "Les épées d'honneur distribuées par les papes pendant les XIVe, XVe et XVIe siècles." *Revue de l'art chrétien* 39 (1889): 408–11, 40 (1890): 281–92.

Pansier, Pierre. "Annales avignonaises de 1370 à 1392, d'après le Livre des Mandats de la Gabelle." *Annales d'Avignon et du Comtat Venaissin* 3 (1914): 5–72.

———. "L'aumône de la Pignote." *Annuaire de la Société des amis du Palais des Papes et des monuments d'Avignon* 23 (1934): 42–61.

Piola Caselli, Fausto. "L'espansione delle fonti finanziarie della Chiesa nel XIV secolo." *Archivio della Società Romana di Storia patria* 110 (1987): 63–97.

———. "L'evoluzione della contabilità camerale nel periodo avignonese." In *Aux origines de l'état moderne*, 411–37.

Prinet, Max. "Les armoiries de Pierre de Cros, archevêque de Bourges." *Mémoires de la Société des antiquaires du Centre* 38 (1917–1918): 59–62.

Renouard, Yves. *Les relations des papes d'Avignon et les compagnies commerciales et bancaires de 1316 à 1378*. Bibliothèque des Ecoles françaises d'Athènes et de Rome 151. Paris, 1941.

Renton, A. W., and G. G. Phillimore. *The Comparative Law of Marriage and Divorce*. London, 1910.

Rey-Courtel, Anne-Lise. "Les cardinaux du Midi pendant le Grand Schisme." In *Le Midi et le Grand Schisme d'Occident*, 49–118. Cahiers de Fanjeaux 39. Toulouse, 2004.

Schwarz, Brigide. "Der *Corrector litterarum apostolicarum*: Entwicklung des Korrektorenamtes in der päpstlichen Kanzlei von Innozenz III. bis Martin V." *Quellen und Forschungen aus italienischen Archiven und Bibliotheken* 54 (1974): 122–91.

Selzer, Stephan, *Deutsche Söldner im Italien des Trecento*. Bibliothek des deutschen historischen Instituts in Rom 98. Tübingen, 2001.

Sickel, Theodor. "Das Vicariat der Visconti." *Sitzungsberichte der kaiserlichen Akademie der Wissenschaften, Philosophisch-historische Klasse*, 30.1 (1859): 3–90.

Soulard, Thierry. "Un inventaire d'orfèvrerie du 14e siècle: l'exécution testamentaire des cardinaux limousins Pierre et Jean de Cros." *Bulletin de la Société archéologique et historique du Limousin* 115 (1988): 52–67.

Thaumas de la Thaumassière, Gaspard. *Histoire de Berry*. 2 vols. Bourges, 1865.

Thibault, Paul R. *Pope Gregory XI: The Failure of Tradition*. Lanham, MD, 1986.

Trexler, Richard C. "A Medieval Census: The *Liber Divisionis.*" *Medievalia et Humanistica* 17 (1966): 82–85.

———. *The Spiritual Power: Republican Florence under Interdict.* Leiden, 1974.

Valois, Noel. "Raymond de Turenne et les papes d'Avignon." *Annuaire-bulletin de la Société de l'histoire de France* 26 (1889): 215–76.

Vingtain, Dominique. *Avignon: Le Palais des Papes.* Photographs by Claude Sauvageot. Le ciel et la pierre 2. No place, no date [1998].

Warren, W. L. "Reappraisal of Simon Sudbury, Bishop of London 1361–1375 and Archbishop of Canterbury 1375–1381." *Journal of Ecclesiastical History* 10 (1959): 139–52.

Weiss, Stefan. "Kredite europäischer Fürsten für Gregor XI.: Zur Finanzierung der Rückkehr des Papsttums von Avignon nach Rom." *Quellen und Forschungen aus italienischen Archiven und Bibliotheken* 77 (1997): 176–205.

Williman, Daniel. "The Camerary and the Schism." In *Genèse et débuts du Grand Schisme d'Occident*, 65–71.

———. "Schism within the Curia: The Twin Papal Elections of 1378." *Journal of Ecclesiastical History* 59 (2008): 29–47.

———. "Summary Justice in the Avignonese Camera." In *Proceedings of the Sixth International Congress of Medieval Canon Law*, ed. Stephan Kuttner, 437–49. Monumenta Iuris Canonici, Series C: Subsidia 7. Vatican City, 1985.

Zutshi, P. N. R. "The Avignon Papacy." In *The New Cambridge Medieval History*, vol. 6: *c. 1300 - c. 1415*, 653–73. Cambridge, 2000.

———. "The Registers of Common Letters of Pope Urban V (1362–1370) and Pope Gregory XI (1370–1378)." *Journal of Ecclesiastical History* 51 (2000): 497–508.

Index

A

Aigrefeuille, Adhémar de, lord of Gramat, 89
Aigrefeuille, Adhémar de, captain of Avignon, 89
Aigrefeuille, Bernard de, bishop of Viviers, 89
Aigrefeuille, Faydit de, bishop of Avignon, 2, 55, 89
Aigrefeuille, Raimond de, 2
Aigrefeuille, Guillaume de, the elder, 89
Aigrefeuille, Guillaume de, the younger, 2, 3, 4, 35, 89
Aigrefeuille, Pierre de, bishop of Avignon, 89
Aigrefeuille, Raimond de, bishop of Rodez, 89
Aix, 81
Albergotti, Giovanni, bishop of Arezzo, 63
Alberti Antichi, bankers of Florence, 33
Albornoz, Gil, cardinal legate, 57
Albornoz, Gomez, vicar of Ascoli, senator of Rome, 58, 85, 86
Allier, river, 1
Amadeo VI, "Green Count" of Savoy, 35, 58, 59, 61, 62, 63
Ameilh de Brénac, Pierre, bishop of Sinigaglia, pope's confessor and librarian, 67, 81–85
Anagni, 5, 19, 67, 69, 70, 86, 87
Ancona, 68, 81–85

Anjou, Louis duke of, 5, 34, 35, 44, 53, 54, 66, 69, 92
Antibes, 82
Aquitaine, 8, 53, 58
Aragon, 29, 82
Arles, 5, 6, 14, 52, 81
Arnanesse, Jacques, procurator fiscal, 22
Arno river, 83
Arsenh, Pierre, bishop of Montefiascone, 84
Astorga, 38
Atbert, Guillaume, clerk of the Camera, 27
Aubert, Arnaud, papal chamberlain, 3, 4, 8, 17–19, 23, 27, 29, 37, 43, 48, 73, 77
Aubert, Etienne: Innocent VI, q.v.
Auch, 5, 43, 91
Aurelianus, first bishop of Limoges, 7
Auriol, 81
Authon, Seguin de, clerk of the Camera, 28
Avignon, 6, 8, 10, 11, 13–15, 18, 21, 23, 24, 27, 28, 30–34, 36, 44, 47–53, 55–57, 60, 62–66, 68–71, 78, 81, 82, 84, 89
Aycelin de Montagu, Gilles, cardinal, 50

B

Balène, Pierre, servant of Pierre de Cros, 15
Bar, Jean de, cubicularius, 83

Barde, Maurice de la, clerk of the Camera, 27, 55
Baroncelli, Giovanni, changer of Avignon, 33, 35
Bassoues, 43
Baucio, Raimond, count of Avellino, 91
Baux, Alix des, 91
Baux, Bertrand des, 56
Baux, Raimond de, viscount of Valernes, 92
Beaufort, Guillaume de, viscount of Turenne, 4, 28, 57, 90–93
Beaufort, Jeanne de, 91
Beaufort, Roger de, 4, 54, 71, 92
Bellemère, Gilles, 5
Benedict XII, pope, 11
Benedictine Order, 1, 2, 10, 12, 36, 43, 91
Béranger, Raimond, master of the Hospitallers, 56
Berry, Jean duc de, 4, 51, 53
Bertin, Guillaume, servant of Pierre de Cros, 15
Bertrand, Pierre, cardinal, 90
Besse, Elise de, 90
Besse, Guillaume de, 8
Besse, Jacques de, 8
Besse, Nicolas de, cardinal, 34, 90
Beaufort, Jean de, archbishop of Narbonne, 83
Blauzac, Jean de, cardinal, 50
Bohemia, 40
Bologna, 6, 30, 57, 59, 62, 63, 65, 69
Bolsena, 33, 85
Bonpas, 50
Bonval, Bernard de, bishop of Bologna, receiver general in Italy, 6, 57, 62
Bordeaux, 54
Borrier, Pierre, clerk of the Camera, 28
Bosmejo, Vital de, collector, 37
Boulogne, Gui de, cardinal, 35, 36

Bourg-sur-Gironde, abbey, 39
Bourges, 3, 4, 5, 10–14, 37, 38, 42, 43, 51
Bozarelli, Agostino, imperial vicar of Pavia, 61
Brandis, Etienne de, admiral of the king of France, 83
Bremen, 10, 38
Bretons, 41, 55, 56, 57, 63, 65, 66, 69, 85
Brioude, 1
Brossano, Simon de, cardinal, 77
Bruges, 32, 33, 55, 67, 91
Bruguerol, Sicard de, councillor of the Camera, 29
Budes, Silvestre, Breton captain, 55–57, 65, 69, 85
Burgundy, 30, 76
Burgundy, Philip duke of, 5

C

Cabassole, Philippe, cardinal, 30, 57, 58
Cabrespi, Jean, councillor of the Camera, 29, 37, 38
Cambarou, Etienne, papal chamberlain, 73
Camerino, Roberto da, 65
Campania, 86
Canilhac, Garine de, 92
Canilhac, Marquis de, 89, 92
Canilhac, Raimond de, cardinal, 35, 92
Capoliveri, 83
Carcassonne, 53, 66
Carit, Bernard, collector, 40
Carpentras, 65, 83, 86, 91
Carrara, Francesco, imperial vicar of Padua, 65
Casilina, Via, 86
Castelnau, Bego de, bishop of Cahors, 53
Castile, 26, 36, 38, 71

Catalans, 82
Cesena, 66, 69
Ceva, Jacopo di, *advocatus Camere*, 23
Chabannes, Adhémar de, 7
Chaise-Dieu, abbey OSB, 36, 89
Chalon, Jean de, prince of Orange, 92
Chambon, Delphine de, 92
Chambon, Marie de, 91, 92
Chanac, Guillaume de, cardinal, 50
Charles II, king of Navarre, 66
Charles IV of Luxembourg, emperor, 30, 52, 59, 61, 65, 66, 74, 76, 77, 85
Charles V, king of France, 5, 11, 28, 40, 41, 54, 66, 70, 83
Chassagne, Pierre de, registrar of papal letters, 83
Chauvigny, Gui de, lord of Châteauroux, viscount of Brosse, 92
Cheylard, Jean de, prior of Charay, deputy rector of the Comtat Venaissin, 56
Chiusi, 60
Choat, Jean, scribe of the Penitentiary, 15
Cistercian Order, 36
Città di Castello, 64
Clement VI, pope, 2, 7–11, 14, 21, 27, 35, 40, 42, 53, 78, 79, 89–92
Clement VII of Avignon, pope, 5, 6, 11, 13, 14, 17, 19, 26–29, 36, 65, 66, 69, 71, 77–79, 89, 91, 92
Clermont, 37
Cluniac Order, 2, 14, 91
Codolet, Raimond de, citizen of Avignon, 15
Comborn, Guillaume de, bishop of Limoges, 90
Comborn, Guiscard de, lord of Treignac, master-at-arms, 85, 90
Comminges, Aliénor de, 91
Comtat Venaissin, 15, 30, 41, 50–52, 55, 56, 57, 91, 92

Constance, Council of, 43
Conzié, François de, chamberlain, 15, 19, 49, 77
Corneto (Tarquinia), 64, 67, 68, 81, 84, 85
Corsini, Pietro, bishop of Florence, cardinal, 3, 84
Coucy, Enguerrand de, 61
Crete, 38
Cros, Bertrand de, cleric of Mende, 3
Cros, Delphine de, 1, 11, 12
Cros, Etienne de, 12
Cros, hamlet, 1
Cros, Pierre de, OSB, bishop of Auxerre, cardinal, 8, 10–12
Cros, Pierre de, abbot of Tournus, 13
Cros, Jean de, bishop of Limoges, cardinal, 1, 4, 6, 11–15, 47, 53, 54, 81, 82
Cros, Hugues de, 11, 12
Cros, Robert de, 12
Cros, Vesian de, chamberlain of S. Victor de Marseille, 13
Crucellis, Gilbert de, 82

D

Dalbiartz, Pierre, clerk of the Camera, 27
Dalmatia, 38
Déaux, Gaucelme de, papal treasurer, 23, 24, 28, 30, 43
Defio, Robert, papal sergeant-at-arms, 83
Denmark, 40
Dieudonné, Jean, commissioner of the Camera, 37, 38
Diseur, Nicolas le, papal secretary, 67, 70
Dominican Order, 3, 7
Durance river, 50, 81
Durançole, water channel in Avignon, 50

E

Edward, prince of Aquitaine and Wales, "The Black Prince", 4, 5, 53, 54, 56
Elba, 68, 83, 84
England and English, 4, 11, 29, 31–33, 36, 37, 53–55, 66, 69, 92
Estaing, Pierre d', archbishop of Bourges, cardinal, 3, 57–59, 63, 69, 84
Este, marquis of: Niccolò, 58

F

Faenza, 66
Fay, Simon le, canon of Bourges, secretary to Pierre de Cros, 13, 29
Fernandez de Heredia, Juan, castellan of Amposta, 41, 56, 81, 85
Ferrara, 58
Ficucchio, Tommaso da, procurator fiscal, 22
Fioule, river, 1
Flandrin, Jean, dean of Laon, archbishop of Auch, 5
Flandrin, Pierre, cardinal, *referendarius*, 4, 64
Florence, 23, 31, 33, 52, 57, 60, 64, 65, 68, 69, 75, 83
Folcaud, Bernard, bishop of Pamplona, 44
Forlì, 66
Fréjus, 82

G

Garde, Catherine de la, 93
Garde, Raymond de la, Latin patriarch of Jerusalem, 5
Garin, Garin, lord of Tournel, 3
Gaston, Philippe de, archbishop of Nicosia, 44
Gaunt, John of, duke of Lancaster, 5, 54

Gazata, Pietro, chronicler of Reggio Emilia, 61, 62
Geneva, Robert of, cardinal: Clement VII, q.v.
Genoa, 68, 82
Gérard, Pierre, bishop of Le Puy, 15
Germany, 27, 28, 36, 37, 40
Gervais, Pierre, collector, 37, 38
Gieri, Cristoforo, changer of Avignon, 33, 35
Gigondas, 56
Giovanetti, Matteo, painter, 8
Girard, Pierre, clerk of the Camera, cardinal, 27, 28
Grailly, Jean de, Captal de Buch, 54
Grange, Jean de la, cardinal, 69, 83
Gregory XI, pope, 4, 7–9, 12–14, 17–19, 23–28, 30, 31, 33, 34, 36–45, 48–51, 53–55, 57, 58, 60, 62, 63, 65–71, 77, 79, 84, 89–97
Grimoard, Anglic, cardinal, 50
Guelph League, 57, 58
Guesclin, Bertrand du, marshal of France, 54, 55
Guesclin, Olivier de, Breton captain, 55, 56
Gui, Bernard OP, 8
Guinigi, bankers of Lucca, 33
Guiraudon, provost of Cavaillon, 83

H

Hauteville, Robert de, captain of mercenaries, 28
Hawkwood, John, condottiere, 55, 59, 61, 64, 65, 69
Hospital of St. John, Order of, 41, 56, 60
Hungary, 40

I

Iberia, 32, 40
Innocent VI, pope, 3, 7, 10, 11, 19, 26, 42, 50, 67, 78, 89, 90

Index

Italy, 3–6, 14, 23, 24, 27, 28, 30, 32, 33, 36, 42, 48, 55–60, 63–71, 76, 77, 79, 91, 92

J

Jean, Pons de, lawyer of Avignon, 49
Jews, 49, 86
Joan of Anjou, queen of Naples, 5, 28, 32, 59, 69, 83, 84
John II, king of France, 35
John XXII, pope, 43, 78
John XXIII of Pisa, pope, 49
Jugie, Hugues de la, bishop of Carcassonne, 53
Jugie, Nicolas de, 90
Jugie, Jacques de, senior and junior, 90
Jugie, Pierre de la, archbishop of Narbonne, cardinal, 35, 53, 60, 82, 83

K

Kent, Joan of, 54

L

Landau, count of, condottiere, 58
Langley, Edmund of, earl of Cambridge, 5, 54
Languedoc, 32, 40, 53,
Laplotte, Pierre de, bishop of Carpentras, *referendarius*, 83, 86
Largier, Bertrand, cardinal, 83
Lateran Council IV, 52
Lefèvre, Pierre, squire, 55
Lérins, 82
Le Puy, 15, 37, 91
Lestranges, Elie, dean of Saintes, 91
Lestranges, Guillaume de, papal chaplain, archbishop of Rouen, 90, 91
Lestranges, Raoul de, papal squire, 12, 55, 89, 91
Limoges and Limousin, 2–15, 38, 41, 53–56, 90–92

Livorno, 82, 83
Lodève, 28
Lombardy, 35, 36, 56, 59, 60, 64
Longanh, Gasbert de, clerk of the Camera, 29
Lordat, Guillaume de, bishop of Lucca, 59
Low Countries, 32
Lucca, 33, 35, 59, 83

M

Mainz, 36
Majorca, 24, 42
Malatesta, Galeazzo, vicar of Rimini, 58
Malestroit, Jean de, Breton captain, 55, 57, 65
Malessec, Guy de, cardinal, *referendarius*, 4, 13
Manrique, Gomez, archbishop of Toledo, 44
Mantua, 18, 59
Marseille, 4, 13, 28, 65, 66, 68, 81–83, 85
Maubert, Jean, collector, 42
Mazel, Bertrand du, collector, 28, 41, 70, 76, 78
Mende, 3, 27, 37, 70
Mercadier, Geraud, chamberlain to Pierre de Cros, 13, 15
Miers, Eblo de, clerk of the Camera, bishop of Vaison, 27
Milan, 59, 61, 62, 65
Mirepoix, 28
Modena, 65
Monaco, 82
Mondragon, castle, 52
Montagu, Gilles Aycelin de, cardinal, 50
Montaurose, Pierre de, collector, 37
Monte Argentario, 84
Montechiari, battle, 61–63
Montefiascone, 3, 28, 30, 48, 64, 67, 84

Montegiorgio, 65
Monteruc, Pierre de, cardinal vice-chancellor, 44, 47, 50, 70
Montesquieu-Volvestre, 52
Montpellier, 23, 28, 69
Moslems, 52
Montmirail, 56

N

Naples, 32, 92
Narbonne, 28, 53, 60, 82, 83, 91
Navarre, 42, 66
Nice, 65, 82
Noellet, Guillaume, cardinal, vicar general, 63, 64
Norfolk, 41
Normandy, 7
Notre-Dame-des-Doms, cathedral of Avignon, 11, 14, 51
Noves, 81

O

Oloron, 52
Orbetello, 83, 84
Orgon, 36, 81
Orléans, 11, 42, 90
Orsini, Niccolò, count of Nola, rector of the Patrimony, 84
Orvieto, 58
Osimo, Niccolò di, papal secretary, 63, 67, 70
Ostia, 63, 67, 68, 85
Otto, duke of Brunswick, 5, 58, 84
Orvieto, 58
Ouvèze river, 57
Oviedo, 38

P

Palaysin, Jean, notary of the Camera, 30
Palestrina, 11, 13, 81, 86
Pamplona, 44
Papal States, 59, 64

Parione, Piazza, 86
Paris, 7, 10, 11, 90
Patrimony of St. Peter in Tuscany, 57, 58, 64, 68, 84
Perrers, Alice, 54
Perugia, 27, 57–59, 64
Pescara, Dondino da, judge of the Temporal Court of Avignon, 56
Philip VI, king of France, 7
Piombino, 68, 83, 84
Pisa, 49, 67, 83
Poissy, Etienne de, cardinal, 35
Poitiers, Aymar de, count of Valentinois, rector of the Comtat Venaissin, 56, 89
Poitiers, Henri de, bishop of Troyes, 91
Poland, 40
Pont S. Esprit, 52
Porta Ostiense, 85
Porta Portese, 85
Port'Ercole, 68, 83, 84
Port-Grimaud, 81
Port-Miou, 81,
Portoferraio, 83, 84
Portofino, 82
Porto Longone or Porto Azzurro, 83
Porto Pisano, 83
Portovenere, 82
Portugal, 36
Posilhac, Giraud de, archbishop of Aix, 81
Pradelle, Raimond de la, archbishop of Nicosia, 44, 60
Prohins, Guillaume de, clerk of the Camera, 28
Prohins, Gui de, knight, senator of Rome, 28, 86
Provana, Jacopo, knight of Turin, 35
Provence, 5, 30, 32, 42, 56, 57, 65, 92
Puy, Gerald du, abbot of Marmoutiers, receiver general, cardinal, 6, 58, 64

Index

R

Raffin, Bertrand, clerk of the Camera, *assignator domorum*, 28, 67, 85
Rais, Jeanne de, 54
Ratonneau, Ile, 81
Reggio, Giovanni da, lieutenant procurator fiscal, 22
Reims, 37, 38, 92
Rhône river, 56, 81
Richard II, king of England, 54
Rimini, 58
Robert, Adhémar, archbishop of Sens, 91
Roche, Catalan de la, changer of Avignon, 15
Roche, Geraud de la, OP, 15
Roche, Gui de la, collector, 44
Roche, Hugues de la, knight marshal of the Curia, 54, 62, 63, 86, 92
Roche, Jean de la, knight, 4, 54, 55, 92
La Rochelle, 70
Rodez, 28, 89, 91
Roger de Beaufort family, 6–10, 13, 30, 31, 34, 89–97
Roger de Beaufort, Guillaume, viscount of Turenne, q.v.
Roger de Beaufort, Jean, archbishop of Auch, 91
Roger de Beaufort, Pierre: Gregory XI, q.v.
Romagna, 57, 63, 66
Rome, 19, 27–29, 34, 51, 64, 66–70, 79, 82, 85, 86, 92
Rousset, Jean, notary of the Camera, 30, 74, 77, 79

S

S. Angelo, Castel, Ponte, 70, 86
S. Cyriaque, 81
S. Flour, 2, 14, 32, 37
S. Giovanni in Laterano, 69, 86
S. Girolamo della Cervaia, 82
S. Liberata, 84
S. Macaire, 55
S. Martial, apostle of the Limousin, 5, 7, 8, 13
S. Martial College Priory, Avignon, 1, 13, 14–16
S. Martial, Hugues de, cardinal, 50
S. Maria Maggiore, 86
S. Maximin, 81
S. Paolo fuori le mura, 85
S. Papoul, 3, 12, 13
S. Tropez, 81, 82
S. Victor de Marseille, 13, 68, 81
S. Yrieix, 55
Sabatier, Jean, secretary and auditor of Pierre de Cros, 13, 15
Sacco del Tronto, battle, 58
Saintes, 70, 90, 91
Salle, Bernard de la, Gascon captain, 55–57, 63, 64, 85
Salon, 5, 14, 68, 81
Sanary-sur-Mer, 81
Sardinia, 32
Sarzana, 69
Savona, 82
Scandinavia, 37
Secondotto, marquis of Montferrat, 58
Segni, 84
Siccacuria, Johannes de, notary of the Camera, 30
Sicily, 27, 36, 41
Solèges, Jacques de, notary of the Camera, 29, 30
Sorgues or Pont-de-Sorgues, 75
Sortenac, Pierre de, cardinal, 13
Spinelli, Niccolò, seneschal of Provence, 65
Sudbury, Simon, bishop of London, 41, 42
Sweden, 40

T

Talamone, 83
Talleyrand de Périgord, cardinal, 7,
Tebaldeschi, Francesco, cardinal, 67, 76
Tici da Pistoia, Andrea, banker of Avignon, 33, 35
Tissanderie, Guillaume de, bishop of Rieux, 90, 91
Tivoli, 69
Tolomei, Cristoforo, proctor of Mantua, 18, 28, 59, 60, 67, 76, 84
Toulouse and Toulousain, 2, 3, 5–7, 12, 43, 53, 70
Tour, Bernard de la, 93
Tour, Guillaume de la, 93
Tour, Jean de la, 93
Tournefort, Jean de, abbot of S. Honorat de Lérins, 82
Trets, 81
Turenne, Nicolas de, 59
Turenne, Raimond de, 15, 59, 85, 86, 89, 91, 92
Turpin, Guillaume, bishop of Angers, 44
Tuscany, 33, 58

U

Urban V, pope, 3, 4, 19, 22–24, 27, 28, 30, 33, 40, 42, 48, 50, 51, 53, 67, 68, 89
Urban VI, pope, 5, 11, 19, 60, 61, 66, 69, 71

V

Vacqueyras, 56
Valmontone, 86
Vatican Palace, 67–70, 85, 86
Venice, 33, 67
Vercelli, 35, 36, 60, 78
Verneuil, Arnold de, collector, 38
Vernols, Pierre de, bishop of Maguelonne, papal treasurer, 15, 23–26, 28, 44
Veyrac, Bertrand de, squire, 55
Veyrols, Geoffroi de, archbishop of Toulouse, 3, 53
Vico, Francesco di, prefect of Rome, 64, 67, 68, 85
Villain de Paris, Pierre, auditor of the Camera, 26
Villefranche, 68, 82
Villemur, Jean de, knight, 4, 54
Villemur, Pons de, bishop of Couserans, 54
Villeneuve-lès-Avignon, 36, 63
Visconti, Bernabò and Galeazzo, 27, 30, 36, 40–43, 52, 57–64, 74, 76
Visconti, Ambrosio, brigand captain, 58
Viterbo, 28, 30, 48, 64, 67, 68, 84
Vodron, Elie de, clerk of the Camera, vice-treasurer, 27, 28, 49, 82, 83
Voute, Aymar de la, bishop of Grasse, 82

Z

Zalva, Martin de, cardinal, *referendarius*, 4